THE

AMERICAN DREAM:

FACTS OR FALLACY?

Why Blame Others For Your Failures

BY

DUDLEY G. EARLINGTON

PublishAmerica
Baltimore

First printing

ISBN: 1-59286-111-3
PUBLISHED BY PUBLISHAMERICA, LLLP
www.publishamerica.com
Baltimore

Printed in the United States of America

FOREWORD

When I was a small boy in the Caribbean, I visualized that one day I would come to America to realize my 'dream.' During my boyhood days, I had a vivid picture in my mind of what America was all about – big houses, big flashy fishtail cars, clean streets, lined with orchids in their splendor, air-conditioned sky-scrapers, where office workers and managers express a sense of gratification in addressing each other by their first names. Crowded shopping malls where people 'shop till they drop.' College campuses where scholars gallivant in academic tranquility and take "no thought for the morrow, for the morrow would take thought for the things of it self." I visualized that in America, people had so much money to spend they had to "sit down on it, "in order to keep it warm.

These vivid pictures of America were a result of my own personal experiences, which were derived from members of my own family, who had travelled to America, as well as information which I obtained from news papers, magazines, and the local press.

Now that I am 'old and gray', and lived in America for thirty years, and have observed the workings of America, I dream of what America could be like and what she should have been in terms of making her vast resources available to her people. I saw the country with my own two eyes, I live in both worlds and I experience both sides of the fence. For some people, the 'American dream' is an illusion; they awake to find an empty space; it is all gone; it was just a night's dream. For others, it is omen, a lovely sight to behold, practical, and full of prosperity.

ACKNOWLEDGEMENTS

Nearly everyone I interviewed for this book is dubious of the popular expression that is called the "American dream." Some people did not even know what the "dream" is, while others have their own notion as to its authenticity.

The phrase, however, is an attestation to the common belief that there is indeed an "American dream" to be fulfilled, and if you educate yourself, adopt good work ethics, and exercise sound planning, the pathway to your 'dream' will be less strenuous.

When I started this book, I had no idea how it would have ended, and did not imagine that so many people have this misconceived notion of the "American dream." To this end, I must express my appreciation to the people (who remain anonymous) for their contribution and their views of the "American dream." Though I cannot list them by name, I hope they will forgive me for not doing so.

However, I am especially grateful to my friend Dana Allen Harris for her unselfish contribution in proofreading the manuscript on a very short notice. For whatever shortcoming or omission this book may contain, I accept full responsibility.

Dudley G. Earlington

TABLE OF CONTENTS

INTRODUCTION

The phrase "the American Dream" has become a typical usage among Americans and also the millions of others who have immigrated to the American shores. For many people, the phrase has been proven to be valid, in one way or another; to others, the term is just a colloquial jargon that fades away during waking hours.

One school of thought believes that "the American Dream" is dying and is now much more difficult to be accomplished. A second school of thought refutes the former, and contends that "the American Dream" is alive and well, and is achievable by all those who pursued it. A third school of thought neither refutes nor accepts the preceding two opposing views, but believes that the American dream is tantamount to hard work. There is even a fourth school of thought that believes that the American dream is an illusion, and never existed for them in the first instance. These opposing views, or rather, these separate viewpoints, will be examined in this book.

"The American Dream" connotes prosperity and a democratic system. That phrase is sometimes used to symbolize the way Americans live and behave in general. The use of the term symbolizes the American nostalgia that reflects on the historical precedents of life in America in general, and the efforts that are being made to promote a suburban value system.

People of all pursuits and with diverse cultural background come to America and blend themselves into a conglomerate with one aim in view, to 'make it big time' in America, and thus fulfill what is called the "American dream." Many people are dubious about the American dream. Some are even reluctant to admit that the 'dream' is an actuality that exists and provides opportunities for all Americans and the millions of others who come to America.

Most people in society have some sort of 'dream,' or goal, that they would like to attain during their lifetime. Some of these aspirations may have been cherished since childhood, some may have been instilled by the parents, while others may have been graphically inspired as a result of the achievements which others have made.

While it is not clear why some people aspire to high achievements (goal-oriented), and others do not, the wide assumption is that everyone wants to be successful. However, not everyone is desirous in doing the things that are necessary and which would ultimately lead to success.

There are also some people in society who believe that it is the responsibility of government to provide for them, and tend to blame their governments, or the unavailability of government's resources, for their failures. It is interesting to note also that some people have come to realize 'their dreams,' but have actually lost it on the wayside because they have become either too relaxed, too complacent, or too repugnantly self-indulgent. Some people believe that the inadequate return for their labor is the result of their low achievements, and that the economic disparity in the American society, which favors one race of people over another race, is a factor which causes their low achievements. Of all the people that I interviewed for this book, the black Americans were the only group that refutes or expresses an uncertain feeling about the reality of the American dream. One such person expressed his feelings in the following manner: "My American dream will not be achieved unless there is equality and justice in America for us blacks.... We see a history of success of the propaganda of the black man,

10

by the white man, about how we are less intelligent than they are.... But we cannot orchestrate a successful propaganda of how the white man robbed us of our labor and resources; we must be compensated for slavery."

These sentiments, along with the views of others, will be explored in an effort to (a) determine whether the phrase "the American Dream" is a visionary reality which is attainable by all Americans and also the millions of others who have migrated to America, or (b) whether the metonym is only an illusion that appeared to be real and reachable when simply viewed, but disappeared when practical methods of achievements are put into practice and (c) how cultural deprivation affect the under-achievements of the black Americans.

As a result of many case studies, the author will try to capture the imagination of his readers and to encourage viewpoints based on practical experiences of those who are pursuing the 'dream.' The author's aim is to embrace the thoughts of the readers of this book in establishing criteria that are employable if one is to fulfill the 'dream,' bearing in mind that the term "the American Dream" is an ideal, a value, which is placed on certain material achievements.

A summation of this text will concisely personify the author's own circumstances as it relates to his American dream, which was inspired in a rural district in one of the Caribbean Islands over five decades ago, and which was inadvertently fulfilled in New York.

CHAPTER ONE
The Pre-sumption

We often hear of the phrase "the American Dream." The phrase denotes how Americans, in general, feel about themselves and the opportunities which the society has provided for them and also for the millions of others who have immigrated to its shores. The Oxford English Dictionary provides us with the following definitions: "The ideal of a democratic and prosperous society which is the traditional aim of the American people; a catch-phrase used to symbolize American social or material values in general."[1]

For some people, the term "the American Dream" is a reality in one form or another; either in economic gains, financial holdings, fame, or political control. For others, the phrase is just a nightmare; empty, worthless, full of tales that fades away in the morning and is forgotten. When an African-American lady was asked what she thinks the American dream is, she replied; "a mule and an acre of land.... That is what it means for us.... It started from way back there; despite all the money that a person may have, if there is no love in the heart (pointing to her heart), there will be no dreams to be fulfilled."

When an African-Caribbean lady was asked the same question, she replied, "The dream is a car in every driveway

---

[1] *The Concise Oxford Dictionary of Sociology*, Gordon Marshal, p 335

and a chicken in every pot … but today, only few driveways have cars and there are not enough chickens to go around."

Generally, the term "the American Dream," which is sometimes loosely used by Americans and also by other people from other countries, tend to symbolize material success (wealth and fame). But the phrase also tends to lend credence to the notion that the only thing that counts in the American society is the dollar ($), (financial gains and economic control),while its democracy and its social values are less exemplified. In any shape or form, the phrase has been proven to be real in many ways, in that the society has enjoyed prosperity in all aspect of developments, and has also enjoyed and is blessed in the abundance of consumer goods and has a history of un-interrupted democratic stability.

While some groups will dispute the authenticity of the social values and economic opportunities for all-Americans, the overall impression is that "the American Dream" is not an imaginary omen, but is an actuality, which can be realized by all Americans who are able-bodied.

We speak of the "American Value System," the standard or status acquired, or the quality of life desired; we also speak of success based on one's achievements; however, success or high achievements are not fixed possessions, and can not be adequately measured with a yardstick. Success or high achievements vary from society to society; what is high standard in some societies may very well be failure and/or under-achievement in other societies. Each society must be examined on the intrinsic nature of its social, economic, educational and political standard in order to be evaluated. To this end, the author will examine:

1. The hierarchy of privileges, which are available to some people within certain ethnic groups in America, based on (a) race, (b) family background, (c) the

occupational status of the parents, and (d) the denial of similar privileges to other groups.

2. The author will also examine the cultural background of various ethnic groups in America, to determine if cultural upbringing affects the eventuality of high achievement among certain classes of people.

3. Also to be examined are the low achievements and the appearance of the lack of motivation (to get ahead) which affects certain classes in America.

4. Whether low rewards and menial positions are consequences of low esteem, thus resulting in the lack of motivation among certain ethnic groups in America.

5. If motivational laxity is a consequence of cultural behavior and if so, whether this cultural behavior is learned or inherited.

These five parts criteria along with the views of others (and their relationship to the American dream) will be discussed in this book.

Society is made up of different types of people; some people will set high goals for themselves, or dream of great expectations or high achievements. The high 'goal-setters' will thrive by the motivation of their desire to get ahead. Armed with this desire and motivation to achieve success, these people will adventurously have their dreams fulfilled and their goals achieved. There are others, however, whose expectations or dreams will turn to nightmares and their goals defeated, particularly if the pathway that leads to these goals are impeded by others, or if resources are unavailable, or if the will-power to remove impediments is compromised, or if the immediate rewards, or incentives are so low and unattractive that the desire to pursue these ends becomes entangled in the pursuit of the dreams and thus loses its zest to continue.

There are a great number of people in America who have lived the American dream through the acquisition of fame and fortune. There are also a great number of people who have had their dreams realized and are living life to its fullest even though they neither acquired fame nor fortune. Some have worked very hard, and for a very long time, in an effort to fulfill their dreams. There are also many people who are born with the knowledge that the finer things in life are provided for them on "platters," attainable at their command. No efforts are being made, no motivation cherished, no sweat to emit; the goals that they set, or the expectations they envision, may have already been placed within their reach, and their dreams are an actuality, by virtue of being born. If they did not succeed, or if they did not attain their goals, it would probably be because of their own choosing; or because they have deviated from the standards or responsibilities which were carved out for them by the society in which they live. Others may fail because of the intervention of fate that invariably may have altered the pathway to their achievements. On a whole, most Americans are of the opinion that there is indeed an "American dream" that is to be achieved.

Also, there are a great number of people of different cultural background and religious persuasions who come to America and blend themselves into this conglomerate of various values in terms of goals to be pursued, or dreams to be fulfilled. Some people come here (to America) with views to express, or impediments to surmount. Whatever the aspirations are, people come to America with the purpose of "making it big," in whatever areas they sought, and thus achieve what is dubbed "the American Dream."

Whether the dream or the goal is plenty of money in the

bank, to have a big house, own a big car, get a good education, have freedom of religion or freedom of expression, experience what constitute democracy, or observe the systematic ingenuity of the workings of capitalism, most of the newcomers have adopted the Americans' idea that there is indeed an American dream to be fulfilled.

People of different pursuit and of different cultural background have unlike expectations in life; they all set their goals according to their desire. There are six different classes of people in society, some of which will be found in any of the following categories:

1. Those who are content with the little or nothing which they have and make no concerted effort to improve their life's situations.

2. Those who would watch others as they succeed, and wonder how, but would make no effort themselves to change their pattern of behavior, or alter their course of direction that would attentively lead to greater achievements; for them, their dreams will eventually fade away.

3. There are some who believe that the society on a whole should make the provisions which are necessary for them to succeed, and that if these provision are not made, they would remain dormant for the rest of their lives and watch as their dreams slowly disappeared into oblivion.

4. There are those who will set goals for themselves, but fail to achieve these goals because of one or more reasons. But these people would sometimes still aspire to some level of achievements which could be considered

reasonable and rewarding; that is, although the desired standard of achievements were not met, they would at least aspire to an acceptable level of accomplishments which would be worthy of consideration.

5. There are others who would set high level of expectations for themselves, but would fail during the process. However, the accomplishments that have been made tend to give a sense of satisfaction and thus compensate for the efforts and the small gain against the failures.

6. Some people contend that they have been trying all their lives to succeed, that they have the desire to get ahead, that they are motivated, but somehow cannot achieve their desired goals; that they need some help, a boast a "jump start." My advise is try harder, you may find that a "bag of gold" is awaiting you somewhere, but you must try.

Once I read a story about a powerful King who put a large rock in the middle of the road to block the way of all who passed by. What the King did not tell anyone, however, was that beneath the large rock was a bag of gold. The people would pass by daily, but instead of rolling away the stone, they would all walk around it, thus creating an alternative pathway.

As the days go by, everyone began to complain about this large rock in the middle of the road; no one, however, made any attempt to roll away the stone. Rolling away the stone would no doubt reveal the bag of gold. After some time had passed, and the complaint continued, the King called some of the peasants and his subjects to the spot where the stone was. The witless indomitable people watched as the King rolled away the large stone to reveal the bag of gold. All the people were astonished when they saw the bag of gold that was hidden under the rock. Everyone then began to cipher to themselves that if they had rolled away the stone, they would have certainly found the bag of gold.

The analogy to this event is that if some people would sometimes take the time, or make the effort to stop and evaluate their life's situation, or try to remove any obvious impediments which hinder their progress or prevent them from pursuing their goals, or fulfilling their dreams, they would probably discover that there is a "bag of gold" that awaits them during the process of their pursuit for a better standard of living.

The American society is composed of a conglomerate of people who are of different ethnic backgrounds, has different aspirations, different cultural upbringings, and also aspire to different kinds of goals in life. Some will reach their goals, or aspire to various degrees of success; but some will also sink to diverse levels of failures. These adventures (whether success or failures), are the result of the opportunities that are opened to those who are successful, or, on the other hand, the lack of these opportunities that are closed to those who failed.

Racial discrimination and economic disparity which exist in America tend to destroy the gleam of expectations for certain ethnic groups in America, thereby diminishing the degrees of achievements, while simultaneously stimulating the expectations of other ethnic groups and thus increasing the intensity of their success and achievements. Based on these analogical notions, I will attempt to draw an inference as to whether "the American Dream" is a reality for all Americans and the millions of others who are fortunate to have embarked on the American shores. An attempt will also be made to determine whether this American dream which is so uncontrollably sought by the Americans is out there somewhere for the 'taking of it,' but has been neglected by some who failed to embraced the opportunities, or who "slept," while the "roll-call" to high achievements went unanswered. .

The author's aim is not an inspiration as to how a "bag of gold" can be found, or any attempt to label any particular behavior as it resolves to economic failure, but only (a) to make an attempt to open the imagination as to whether "the American Dream" can be realized by all Americans or (b) whether the pathway that leads to success is equally available to all Americans, to be utilized to its fullest, by all Americans, and which could invariably lead to one's level of expectation.

Also to be examined is whether "the American Dream" can be fully realized by the millions of others who have emigrated to the United States of America from other countries in search of "greener pastures" and to fulfill their dreams. I will then leave this open question to the imagination of the readers of this book, who will retrospectively draw their own conclusions and hence be the 'judge.'

Mobility Versus Rewards

Social Scientists defined social mobility as the process by which people in society move either upward or downward in their careers. Social mobility runs either vertical or horizontal.

Vertical mobility tends to involve millions of people and their families who are inclined to adjust their status and to ascend the career ladder.

Sociologists have determined that social mobility is a movement which people experience during their individual careers – they move either upward, or downward, as on a staircase, or as on an elevator.

Horizontal mobility is a process by which millions more people will travel over the ocean to other countries in search of a better life. While the writer will not refute these main focuses of sociologists, namely, vertical and horizontal mobility, it is necessary to add to these two components parts of mobility, another process which I will call circular mobility. Circular mobility is a process by which people move around in circular motions; that is they neither move upward nor downward; they have no careers, and they do not seek careers; they remain stagnant and stationary throughout their adult life; their life's situations do not change. They do the same things (nothing) from day to day. They wake up in the morning and they eat; they gallivant throughout the remainder of the day, doing very little or next to nothing to enhance their economic, social, or educational standard. They eat and go to beds at nights with no agenda for the morrow.

Tomorrow comes, and the prior days non-agenda is repeated. This is the cycle that perpetuates the life's span of the circular mobile, their life's situation does not change. In actuality, they contribute nothing towards the society in which they live; they make no decisions; they sow not, and they do not reap; they seek not, and they do not find; they are therefore not socially mobile.

Sociologists have never ever mentioned the existence of such groupings within the society. In actuality, it is my view, that if one is not moving upward, nor downward within the society, then you must be moving in a circular motion

Daniel Bertaut in *Dentins Personnels et Structures de Classes* (Paris, 1997) studied the class structures of society and arrived at the undeniable conclusion "that all class position should be understood as trajectories...." and that "a given slot may be linked to multiple potential trajectories."[2]

He further stated that "one of the critical aspects of a class structure ... is, how it spreads out over the life cycle and how it is distributed in the population." Continuing, he said that "it is not a simple recasting of the old problems of social

---

[2] Wright, Erik Olin. *Class, Crisis and The State*, Verso Edition London, 1978 p. 93

mobility."[3]

Bertaut implied that many job changes which look like mobility are not mobility at all (high or low) but merely different phases of a single trajectory.

The only genuine mobility, he said, "would be situations in which individuals move from one trajectory to another."[4]

In my view, circular mobility or circular motion merely implies that some sort of movements are taking place within the economic structures of certain members, or groups within the society, but that this movement is not necessarily going upward nor downward.

While the "sky is the limit" for those who are upwardly mobile, in terms of ascending the career ladder, and 'rock-bottom' is the lowest ebb for the downwardly mobile, who has no further to go, the circularity mobile has nowhere to go, except to go around in circles, because they neither go up nor down. It is therefore not a coincidence that those who fall into these categories are the poor and needy, the ignorant, the feebleminded, the uneducated, and the impoverished.

Pitrim Sorokin (1927) in *Social Mobility* contended that the channels of vertical circulation exist in any stratified society and are necessary as channels for blood circulation in the body. In addition, he stated that the staircase or elevator is necessary to the efficient allocation of talents to occupations and that failure to achieve this, tends to promote inefficiency and disorder. Sorokin examined the hierarchy of privilege, the mobility between family of origin and one's own status position. He concluded that the role of educational achievements as compared to that of the social background, or ascription such as race or ethnic background, leads to

---

[3] Wright, Erik Olin *Loc. Cit.*

[4] Wright, Erik Olin *Loc. Cit.*

occupational attainment. He maintained that schools function primarily as "a testing selecting and distributing agency and encourage the development of talents."[5] Sorokin alluded to the fact that some sociologists viewed mobility in the context of hierarchy in which the individual can be ranked according to income, education, and attainment of social prestige, while others set mobility (upward or downward) in the context of a class structure.

Researchers studied the extent to which the occupational status of individuals is associated with the status of the families rather than by individual achievements such as education or attainment. They also studied the relationship between father and son (the link between occupational success), and concluded that the children's occupational success mostly operates through the educational attainment of the parents.

In analyzing the class system of the society, researchers assumed that individuals are born into a distinctive social class, whose membership tends to be lifelong.

Kingsley Davis and Wilbert Moore in their research on mobility concluded that rewards are necessary to motivate individuals to undertake training for functionally important positions in society; hence the assumption that those members of society who are not born into distinctive social class must therefore undergo training in order to realize their dream.

After the depression of the 1930s, the American society has gone through a great transformation. This transformation has virtually influenced all functional aspects of the society, including modern democracy, which is the working knowledge of the American capitalistic system.

Technological advancement and industrial expansion are also the derivation of this transformation. The correlation

---

[5] Merton, Robert and Nisbet, Robert *Contemporary Social Problems*, Harcout, Brace & World, Inc. 1971 p.p 55-56

between technological inventions and industrial expansion has had an implacable and violent effect upon social equality and economic parity in the American society. The force of industrial expansion in the American society is interrelated in one form or another in the process of social mobility.

Robert K. Merton and Robert A. Nisbet in *Contemporary Social Problems* contended that "one important element of social mobility is that the process tends to break the stronghold of isolation, economic isolation, and social isolation;"[6] and that struggle to succeed between individuals and groups has become a way of life in the society. As a result of this struggle, the subsequent economic and social success of certain ethnic groups in America has become, as it were, imminent and compelling.

Merton and Nisbet maintained that, for some individuals, the struggle lies behind some great achievements, but for others, the struggle lies behind tragedies. For example, tragically, some will deviate from the standard and norms of the society and will resort to means that will not be tolerated by the society. The selling of drugs, or engagement in organized crime, prostitution, or other forms of deviant behavior are some of the areas this group will resort to in order to fulfill their dreams.

All these deviant behaviors are exhibited in the name of social mobility. Thus, the struggle to achieve an upward mobility status has been castrated and is a reflection on the moral values within the American society. On the other hand, those who (for one reason or another) cannot attain their goals by any means, or have their dreams realized in any way, shape, or form, are doomed to economic, social, and psychological frustration.

------

[6] Merton, Robert & Nisbit, Robert Op. Cit. p.p 21,23

The cumulative results of the computer revolution and advance technology has had a profound effect and has impacted greatly on the social and economic life of Americans on a whole. The computer revolution, the worldwide use of the internet in the area of commercial networking and the distribution of goods and services, have now become the fundamental aspects of the way towards achieving the American dream. The fallacy of the chicken-in-the-pot-and-car-in-the-driveway is now embedded in the impending reality of a computer in every home and knowledge of the internet.

In the final chapter, I will make an attempt to provide some insight into a series of steps which, in my opinion, are necessary for one to follow, in an effort to achieve his or her goal, or to have his or her American dream realized.

There is, however a word of caution which should be strongly emphasized: many immigrants who come to the United States of America, and a great many more who are anxious to come, are of the opinion that the streets of America are paved with gold and are there for the "taking of it."

There is no such entity; there is no "bag of gold" hidden anywhere in America. One's expectation can be realized, and one's dream can be fulfilled; the process that leads to these achievements is outlined in the summary and final chapter of this book. Each subject matter is outlined in the graph in figure 1. These eleven-part concepts are necessary, and if they are carefully followed, they will eventually lead to the acquisition of high achievements.

CHAPTER TWO
Is The American Dream
Available To All Americans?

In Chapter One, it was mentioned that "the American Dream," in its classical sense, symbolizes the importance that Americans in general place upon the social and material values of the society. It was also mentioned that while many Americans have fulfilled and are living and enjoying their American dream to its fullest, there are many others who also believe that the "American dream" does exist, but have yet to realize what it really is.

While there are many who believe that the 'dream' can only be achieved through the intervention of government with financial assistance and other relief methods, there are many others who believe that the 'dream' is only a nightmare, and that it is only available to a special class of people.

It was also mentioned that people of all persuasions, with different cultural backgrounds, would set different kinds of goals for themselves, and that they (the goal-seekers) would aspire towards their individual set goals according to the avenues or opportunities that are available to them. That there are others who, although the avenues to their success seem to be blocked, or far-reaching, they would make every effort, untie every knot, remove all conceivable barrier in order to succeed. They do not sidestep the barrier, nor relinquish the hope, but would use all available means, find the most accessible trail, or employ the wits that are necessary to manage any seemingly insurmountable task, in order to remove the obstacles or impediments, thus making their dreams an eventuality. Based on this basic premise, I will make an attempt to examine the underlying assumption that there is an "American dream" to be fulfilled, and assuming that this is so, is it available to all Americans, and how can one go about achieving it.

Different Folks Different Strokes

In an attempt to establish certain premises as to how Americans in general feel about "the American Dream" on a whole, case studies were done in the New York, New Jersey, Connecticut, and Baltimore area, where a number of people were asked whether they believed in "the American Dream" and if they believed that the "dream" was available to all Americans.

New York City (where most of the interview was conducted), was particularly chosen because it is considered the "melting pot," where a vast cross section of people come from all over the world in order to realize their dreams. The sample consisted of thirty-five people, all of whom were either self-employed or employed by someone else. The people who were interviewed were of different cultural backgrounds. Some were born in America (Americans) and some were born in foreign countries. Some were white Americans and some were other whites who were born in other countries. Some were black Americans and some were other blacks from the Caribbean or from Africa. Others were of various ethnic backgrounds, such as Arabs, Latinos, Asians, and so on. The people interviewed had various levels of education. Some were college-educated, some had skilled training, such as trade school training, beauty school training, mechanical training, or 'on-the-job-training.' Some had no formal training other than work experience training which they acquired during the course of their employment.

*

J.M. is a black American female in her early 40s. She was employed as an administrative secretary at a government agency.

Interviewer: "Do you believe in the "American dream?
J.M.: "Yes, I believe in the dream, but my "American dream" is yet to be fulfilled.
Interviewer: "What is your "American dream?"
J.M.: "My "American dream" is to have enough money so I can leave this place (referring to her job) and I don't ever have to work again; that's my dream."
Interviewer: "Do you think you'll ever get enough of it?"
J.M.: "I don't think I'll ever get enough from this job, but I'll certainly try. What's the American dream anyway? I have my house already, I have a car, I have a job, I went to college, is that it? No, it's got to be more to it, that can't be it." (She laughed heartily).
Interviewer: "You are right, there is more to it."
J.M.: "What is it?"
Interviewer: "Well, the "American Dream" entails the aim of the American people in terms of its social and material values."
J.M.: "You see, that's what I mean; Americans place so much emphasis on material things and yet about 20% of its people are living in poverty, how do you like that?"
Interviewer: Are you saying then that the dream is not available to all Americans?"
J.M. "That's what I am saying; and it's a shame; because this country has so much; but until America eradicates racism, (economic racism, and social racism), only certain people will ever fulfill their dreams."

*

P.J. is a black American male in his late thirties. He has a college degree and is employed as a human services inspector in a government agency.

Interviewer: "What is the American dream, and do you believe in it?"

P.J.: "Yes, I believe in the American dream, but for me, "the American Dream" is a two-fold question.   First, there is the moral question and second, there is the economic question....

You see, when we talk about the "dream," or "my dream," or "the American Dream," some people might shoot for the moon and reach the stars; others may shoot for the stars and reach the moon. It all depends on who you are or where you are from."

Interviewer: "Could you elaborate on that?"

P.J.: "Sure; It is nice to have a big house and a nice car, education, money in the bank, and a family, but for me, "the American Dream" or "my American dream" is to see that all black people are liberated; then my dream would be fulfilled."

Interviewer: "How do you plan to accomplish that moral question regarding your dreams given the odds?"

P.J.: "What odds? There are no odds, all we have to do is create outlets; that is why I am involved in the computer chip business, so that I can create avenues of economic liberation. After the economic liberation is created, then the other parts of the dream can easily be accomplished."

*

M.A. is a female Latino who was born in a foreign country. She was schooled in an American University and works as a social worker. She was not sure what "the American Dream" was.

M.A.: "What is the 'American dream?' Is it to buy a big house, a nice car, and to get a college education? …If that is the dream, then I guess you could get all of that in your own country."

Interviewer: "But you left your own country and came to America, schooled yourself in America, and now you are employed in America, therefore there must be something about America; don't you think so ?"

M.A.: "Yes, I believe so; I believe that it is the opportunities that are available to everyone why we all come here … the opportunities are there but sometimes the end results are not so great, you have to work hard for it."

*

R.S. is a black American female in her early thirties. She said she has one son but she is not married.

Interviewer: "Do you believe in the American dream?"

R.S.: "It's funny that you should ask me that question just one week before my graduation."

Interviewer: "Where are you graduating from?"

R.S.: Manhattan Community College after four agonizing years, I am so tired."

Interviewer: "So that is one major part of realizing the 'American dream;' right?"

R.S.: "That is it? To be graduating from college?"

Interviewer: "Yes, that is part of it, wouldn't you say?"

R.S.: "It might be part of it but I still don't believe in the American dream."

Interviewer: "Why not?"

R.S.: "Because it is an illusion."

Interviewer: "Why do you say that?"

R.S.: "Because of the nature and the workings of the American society."

Interviewer: "Could you elaborate on that, please?"

R.S.: "Sure, until America find a cure for racism in this society, there will be no dream for people like me.... A dream should be a good thing, right? Joyful, pleasant, and something to wake up to; but it is not so in America. The future for us blacks is like a dreaded nightmare.

Interviewer: "But some dreams are good, and some are bad, right?"

R.S.: "Agree."

Interviewer: "So it will not always be joy in the morning, don't you agree?"

R.S.: "America legislates racism and discrimination against the black race in America, so there is no American dream to be fulfilled for us; but catch me after graduation, we will talk some more."

*

G.E. is a black female in her early sixties who was born in the Caribbean. She is employed in a government agency. G.E. completed post graduate studies in America, but went to college in her own country before she came to the United States. She owns her own house but has no cars, although she previously owned three cars before they were all stolen. Her three children were schooled in America from elementary to college.

Interviewer: "Do you believe in the American dream?"

G.E.: "No, I don't believe in it, what is it anyway?"

Interviewer: "How can you say that you don't believe in it if you do not know what it is?"

G.E.: "Is it to own a house, have a big car, a family, and money in the bank? If this is so, then these things can also be achieved in your own country."

Interviewer: "That might be so, but did you achieve those things before you came to America? And if so, why did you come?"

G.E.: "Well, there are more opportunities, including education in this country (America)."

Interviewer: "So you do believe that there is an "American dream" to be fulfilled?"

G.E.: "Well, let me put it this way, one of the reason why people come here thinking that there is an 'American dream' is because of the democracy and its high regard for family values. They (the Americans) place a high regard on the family. You see, a lot of countries have some form of dictatorship or communistic system, and the people who get ahead are those who were born in certain families or belong to certain lineage. There is a democratic system here and the opportunities are open to everyone. People come here (to America), work and save their money, and then go back to their country and flaunt it, giving others the impression that there is gold on the streets of New York, but I don't believe in the dream."

*

D.H. is a Chinese American who has a college degree and is employed as a computer technician.

Interviewer: "Do you believe in the "American dream?"
D.H.: "Which is?"
Interviewer: "Have you ever heard of the term the "American dream?"
D.H.: "Yes, I've heard of it; when one speaks of "the American Dream," I believe that it is to own a house."
Interviewer: "So is there an American dream?"

D.H.: "It depends on your concept of what the dream is. Some people have different dreams, but the condition now in America does not afford people to fulfill their dreams."

Interviewer: "Do you think "the American Dream" is over-emphasized, or do you believe that it is available to all Americans?"

D.H.: "I do not think it is over-emphasized, but as I said before, things have changed. For example, I have a house, I have a family, I have two cars, my oldest daughter is in college, but young people who are now graduating from college, they expect to get a good job and have a house of their own or get an apartment, but most of them are still living in their parents' house. That was not their dream!"

Interviewer: "But a dream is not something that is fulfilled overnight, it is something that one would have to pursue or work toward; don't you agree?"

D.H.: "Yes, I agree, but let us take another scenario, some people are trapped in the ghetto all their lives; a few may have their American dream come true by moving out of the ghettos; as a matter of fact, that might be their only dream to separate themselves from ghetto life, but what about the millions who have no hope of moving out, their dream is a nightmare which cannot be attained."

Interviewer: "Are you saying then that "the American Dream" is geared for only a selected few?"

D.H.: "That is putting it mildly, because some people do not even think that there is an "American dream," much less to try to attain it.... Some people set goals for themselves but never achieve it because they set too high a standard for themselves which is unattainable or unreachable."

Interviewer: "But don't you think that if people set goals for themselves they should work toward that goal in order to achieve it?"

D.H.: "Yes, but circumstances and other obstacles sometimes prevent people from achieving that which they were aiming for."

Interviewer: "What do you think one should do in a situation of that nature?"

D.H.: "Well, if you set a goal for yourself, or have a dream of being successful in certain aspects of life, then you should work toward that which you have aspired, but as I have said before, some people will not aspire to anything."

Interviewer: "Do you think that these people should just "give up" and stop dreaming?"

D.H.: "You can't stop someone from dreaming, what really counts is the effort that one engenders to make that dream come true and also the end result, only time will tell."

*

C.P. is a black American male in his early 40s. His parents were born in the West Indies and came to the United States in the late 50s. C.P. manages a family business with his mother.

Interviewer: "Have you ever heard of the term the "American Dream?"

C.P.: "Yes, I have, what about it?"

Interviewer: "Do you believe in it?"

C.P.: "Yes, I do."

Interviewer: "Do you think it is achievable by all Americans?"

C.P.: "Everyone should have an imagination as to what they want to be in life. However, there will be roadblocks, but that does not mean that you should stop trying. You can make any amount of money that you want to make in this country (America). Foreigners come here and they make a lot of money and are doing good; there is no gold on the streets of New York, but if you really want to make it, you can."

Interviewer: "Why do you think some people fail?"

C.P.: "Either that they don't have any motivation, they are lazy, or they are too educated."

Interviewer: "What do you mean by "too educated?""

C.P: "You see, if you are too educated, you put a ceiling on yourself or on your education; you have to be flexible and do other things."

Interviewer: "If education is one of the goals, why do you think that too much education is bad?"

C.P : "Look on these young kids out there playing basketball and are making millions of dollars. They go to college but all they do is "play ball," they don't learn a thing; at least most of them, but they fulfill their "American dream," this is what we call – America."

*

S.W. is a Jewish male in his early forties. He is college-educated and is employed by the government. He is single, When asked if he believed in "the American Dream," S.W. replied, "Oh yeah, but you can't sit on your butt and get it. That was the standard of the Founding Fathers, that every American should strive to the top, be the best you can, and even if you do not reach the top at least you would have reached halfway."

Interviewer: "So do you think the dream is available to all Americans?"

S.W.: "Look, man, a lot of people 'hang out' on the street corner and say that America is unjust to them. If you are lucky enough to win the lotto, fine, good luck to you; but it's a long shot and in order to win you have to play the game. If you are disabled and can't work, I'll sympathize with you; but if you are strong and healthy, there is no reason why you can't achieve your goal – this is America, the land of prosperity, if you can't make it here, you won't be able to make it any other place."

*

T.C. was born in Asia, he came to the United States when he was twenty-five (25) years of age. He is now fifty (50) years of age. He said he attended an American University and is employed as an accountant.

Interviewer: "Do you believe in the "American dream?"

T.C.: "The American dream? To be living in America is a dream in itself.... How do you define "the American Dream" anyway?"

Interviewer: "It is the traditional aim of the American people which symbolizes, in part, material values."

T.C.: "Well, in that case I do believe in it, but you have to work hard for it, unless you were born in a privileged class. You see, "the American Dream" is not for everybody."

Interviewer: "What do you mean, it's not for everybody?" I thought it was the aim of all Americans?"

T.C.: "Yes, it is the aim of all the American people, and those people who come here from other countries like you and me. But some people are not going to achieve anything. You have to understand that you have to want something in order to get something."

Interviewer: "Are you saying then that those who failed to achieve success did not want to be successful?"

T.C.: "I am not saying that, but there are lots of opportunities in this country (America) for everyone, but not everyone is taking advantage of it. I dreamt of coming to this country (America) since I was a small boy back in.... (country is omitted). I am here; so even if I don't get rich, at least I have accomplished most of my dreams, including getting a college education.... Just to be here in America is a part of my dream and if I live long enough, I'll get all the material things that I want."

*

S.B. is a black American female who has a college degree and is employed as a social worker at a city hospital.

Interviewer: "Do you believe in the "American dream?"
S.B.: "If I believe in it? Are you kidding me? This country has discriminated against me all my life, the generation before me, and also those before them, for three hundred years; we, the African Americans, are just beginning to see a little light at the end of the tunnel, that is just a crumb from the master's table. Until we (black Americans) have enough money and control some of the major corporations and are able to determine our own destiny, there will be no American dreams for us (blacks). So don't ask me about 'American dream,' it is not for us blacks, it is a white concept which is only accomplished by white people, not black people."
Interviewer: "Are you saying that no black person has been able to realize the American dream?"
S.B.: "I am not saying that, but the majority of us are poor, and many of us are living below the poverty line; what we call economic inequality. This is a racist country and until America gets rid of racism, there will be no 'American dream' for us."

*

J.B. is a black female who came to America from the West Indies in the latter part of the 1960s. She had no formal education beyond primary school. J.B. worked as a nurse's aide in a nursing home during the day and at nights she took care of an elderly woman who is disabled. After about six months she saved enough money to sponsor her husband from the West Indies to America. Her husband had not completed primary school education but back in his native land he had his own business. J.B.'s husband quickly found a job (with the help of a friend) as a maintenance help, but a few months later, he found a more prestigious position as a security guard at a neighborhood bank. He worked at the same job for twenty-four (24) years. When he passed away a few years ago (the victim of cancer) he left to his wife and children three homes fully paid for. One of the homes were bought for cash, out of his 401K Pension Plan.

J.B. said (when asked if she believed in "the American Dream"), "I firmly believe in it, and those people out there who complain that they can't find work, it's because they are lazy and don't want to work, they expect the government to 'mind' them." Then she said; "I can use my husband as an example; he came to America when he was 40 years old and fulfilled his 'American dream;' he died and left me and I don't have to worry about where the next meal is going to come from. I tried to instill in my children every day that they should make good of themselves and take advantage of all the opportunities that America has to offer them; thank God every one of them are doing very well, except....(name withheld) because she went astray and married a black American. She had a house, she had her nice car, she had a good job, and now she has nothing ; the government is now paying her rent and he is in jail.... You can be what you want to be in this country (America)."

Self-Driven Versus Self-Contentment

On March 10, 1998, the Blockbuster award was given out on national television. One of the winners, who was born in a foreign country, expressed his appreciation to the large audience for voting for him. As he spoke, he reflected on the days when he was a small boy in a little village in his country watching movies and wished and hoped that one day he would get the chance to come to America to act in one of those movies. He got his chance; and in his closing remarks he stated that America is the land of opportunity and that anybody can be what they want to be if they so desire. "Don't let anyone tell you that you can't do it," he said, "all you kids out there, you can do it too, you can all be what you want to be."

I once had a friend who came to the United States from the West Indies in the 1960s on a visitor's visa. Years ago when I first met him he had recently returned from the Vietnam war and was attending college at nights. I met this young man, whom I will call John, at a social gathering in the summer of 1970.

During a discussion, he told me that he is a veteran and that he was going to college at nights to get a degree in Business Administration. At the time he was employed at a bank in a training program. At the time, I asked him how long he had lived in America and if he had liked the country. In the 1960s and 1970s, one of the typical questions that a "West Indian" would ask another "West Indian" whom they met was, "how long are you here?"

"So how long are you here?" I asked.

John did not answer the question directly; "Man, I am a veteran," he said with certain amount of confidence in his voice.

I was astonished, but I tried to hide my astonishment. "You are a veteran, how on earth did you become a vet?" I asked, still surprised.

"I am a citizen of the United States, but at the time, I did not even have a green card. I just came back from Vietnam," said John.

"Vietnam?" I asked with much amazement. "How did you get into Vietnam, coming from the West Indies?" I asked, astounded.

"Boy, it's a long story," John remarked, "but I'll make it as quick as possible, because I have to pick up my wife at the subway station." He told me that he came to the United States on a visitor's visa in the late 1960s; he over-stayed his visa and did not return to his country, because, as he bluntly puts it: "I did not have anything to go back to, and since I was already here (in America), I had to find a way to stay in the country; so I registered in the army."

"And they took you without a green card?" I asked.

John: "Yeah, I told them (the recruiters) that I didn't have one, but that I wanted to serve; the man said to me, 'No problem, soldier,' so I knew I was in."

"Just like that?" I asked,

"Just like that," he replied.

"They did not care who you were or where you come from at that time, they were desperate for people to serve and to go to Vietnam, and would have done anything to get me. About two weeks later I was in South Carolina undergoing training and two months later I was shipped off to Vietnam as a citizen of the United States."

"Man," I said, "I am glad that you came back alive, but why did you do it?"

John stared me in the face for two or three seconds then he said, "Boy, I did it so I could help my mother, that's the only way I could have helped her to come to this country, and I have no regrets about it, this is a land of opportunity.... Catch you later."

John might have exaggerated the time span between the time he was inducted into the army and the time that he actually went to Vietnam, but the courageous decision by this young man to join the United States army, when so many young American men were "dodging" the draft, in an effort to avoid going to Vietnam, was very compelling and must be viewed with loyalty, and has exemplified the quest for achieving the American dream, at any cost.

The courage by this "West Indian" demonstrated a clear obscuration of the danger of fighting in Vietnam, and the fear of not returning home to sponsor his mother from the West Indies is worthy of the highest praise for a man who was self-driven to pursue his American dream.

The name John is a pseudonym to hide the identity of the person involved.

Self-Content

Some mundane scholars contend that "theAmerican dream is out of reach for millions of Americans...." and that, despite hard work, this generation of Americans now finds themselves outside of the mainstream of the pathway that would ostentatiously lead to the fulfillment of their dream. Others contend that they have been working all their lives and yet they are unable to realize what the American dream is all about.

Before a game of baseball, or a game of cricket (British) is started, the potential players must practice in order to get themselves in shape or to enhance their confidence for the real game. On the other hand, the field must be prepared in order to protect and to provide the players with the best safety possible. In real-life situations, it is necessary for individuals to first educate themselves, and motivate themselves for the task ahead; then focus on the goals they expect to reach, or the dreams to be fulfilled. Education does not necessarily come from the classroom, but from life's experiences. All these preparation require not only hard work, but also a certain kind of behavior pattern.

A woman in her late 40s remarked that when she was growing up she told her mother that she wanted to be a nurse and to help people; but instead, "I ended up in the kitchen as a kitchen help in a restaurant. God knows that I tried but I just could not make it beyond the 8th grade. My mother was on welfare," she said. "I ended up on welfare too when I had my first child; but later, I had to take a job because I didn't want to end up living like my mother.... This is not what I wanted to do, but times were hard then, it is still hard for us (black Americans)."

Some people would argue that the social economic and democratic system in America favors one race over another and is therefore flawed; frankly, there is no dispute. But if each individual would take some responsibility for their own lackadaisical behavior in the society in which they live (both socially, economically, and financially) they would find great enhancement and make great improvement in their lives.

Try a little harder, comrade, Rome was not built in one day, there is still time. Bear in mind the Chinese Proverbs that "a thousand miles begins with the first step."

CHAPTER THREE
The Two Faces Of "Uncle Sam"

I often wondered, why is it that economic discrimination, poverty, and ignorance continue to plague America, although the country has made so much economic progress and continues to prosper over and beyond all other major industrial nations?

America has survived the depression of the 1930s-1940s and has surged ahead economically, especially since the 1960s. In spite of this prosperity, poverty, economic disparity and ignorance continues to exist in America, "big time."

Peter Clecak, in his book *American Quest For The Ideal Self*, stated that "...the quest for individual fulfillment can be conducted with reasonable prospects of success within a wide range of material, social and cultural circumstances."[1] He further stated that "what individuals require minimally is ... a piece of social justice and cultural space that in their view is sufficient to enable them to pursue their desperate images of salvation."[2] Clecak, in elucidating his point-of-view, stated that "he referred not only to social class, but also ... to the dominant cultural images and imperatives that hamper citizens in their

---

[1] Peter Clecak, *American Quest For The Ideal Self*, New York, Oxford University Press 1983, p14

[2] Peter Clecak, *Loc. Cit.*

quest for fulfillment."[3]

The lower echelon of the American society contends that because of the social and economic injustice in America, they are unable to pursue their goals in life, or have their dream fulfilled, and that their social and economic expectations are not only narrow and rigid, because of this injustice, but is also bombarded by racial prejudice and discrimination.

The majority of the American people were born into distinct social class and thus have their American dream reserved for them. The minority who were not born into this distinct class must undergo training in order to realize their dreams. Interestingly, even though some members of the minority class have fulfilled the training and have prepared themselves educationally for the task, racial discrimination has become an impediment and has played a major role in the prevention of realizing the dream.

David Farber, in his book *The Age of Great Dreams*, epitomize America's great challenge as a fixable element in the executive branch of the federal government. Faber stated that the late President "Lyndon B.Johnson wanted to use the power of the federal government to build a society where the demand of morality ... could be realized in the life of the nation."[4] He further stated that "America's great challenge as seen" by the late President "was domestic, racial discrimination and poverty."[5]

In an effort to embellish the political philosophy of the late President, Farber described him as a "true liberal democrat,

---

[3] Peter Clecak, *Loc. Cit.*

[4] Faber, David *The Age of Great Dreams*, Hill & Fang – A Division of Faber, Strauss & Girout, NY 1994 P.104

[5] Faber, David *Loc. Cit.*

who believed that the federal government was endowed with the responsibility to reduce inequality and to protect and provide for minorities who have been historically oppressed,"[6] and that Johnson dreamt that all those things could be realized in the American society. In his effort to fulfill these dreams, Johnson "passed consumer protection acts, mass-transit aid, antipoverty programs, health measures ... Arts and Humanities, consumer and work place protection acts, aid to higher education...."[7] and many more.

Johnson's White House Staff Assistance for Domestic Affairs put it bluntly: "We simply could not accept poverty, ignorance, and hunger as intractable permanent features of American society. There was no child we could not feed, no adult we could not put to work, no disease we could not cure, no toy, no food, or appliance we could not make safer, no air or water we could not clean."[8]

Incidentally, the Johnson war on poverty did not accomplish all that it was designed to do. CAP (Community Action Program), which was implemented to train and educate minorities, was inadvertently misguided into the wrongful hands of community interest groups who were seeking to satisfy their own immediate individual needs. Instead, the administration of these programs should have been directed and run by local government agencies under the watchful eyes of Federal authorities.

In addition to the programs mentioned (above), there were the "housing acts, school bills, pre-school bills, rent supplements, medical assistance programs, legal aid, food and

---

[6] Faber, David *Op. Cit.* p.105

[7] Faber, David *Loc. Cit.*

[8] Faber David *Op. Cit.* 106

meal subsidies, and delinquency prevention programs. Supplements to social security benefits were expanded and the welfare programs were also expanded."[9] But in spite of all these anti-poverty programs, poverty and ignorance continue to exist in America.

Some people believed that the best way to eradicate poverty and ignorance in the society was to "give money to the poor by taking it from the rich," or to increase the taxes on the rich, which they called *wealth redistribution.* The Johnson administration, however, did not believe that this was the best solution to combat poverty. Johnson stated, "We want to offer the forgotten fifth of our people opportunity, not doles."[10]

The question now arises, how can a country with all this wealth eradicate poverty from the society? Some radical groups argued that the most advantageous way to do away with "poverty in America was to have the poor people themselves decide the means by which they could"[11] relieve themselves from this chronic situations, and that this could be done through the medium of Community Action Programs. The plan was to empower the federal government to provide the means, but the poor themselves would decide what programs would do them the most good. The government caved in and CAP was implemented; but although this venture appeared to have had some merit, the most astounding aspect of this implementation was that community activists and community residents began to "take charge" and the concerted efforts of the late President to end poverty in America did not only fail, but it was a natural disaster.

---

[9] Faber, David *Loc. Cit.*

[10] Faber, David *Loc. Cit.*

[11] Faber, David *Loc. Cit.*

But Johnson did not give up, he was determined to end poverty in America one way or the other, and so, in an effort to do so, he subsequently expanded other social programs such as food stamps, Assistance to Family with Dependent Children (AFDC) and also "free school meals." He also expanded the Medicaid bill, which provided health care for millions of poor people who had no previous coverage.

No one would dispute the fact that these programs did indeed help the poor and provided some temporary stop gap measures to those who were in dire need, but the people who derived the most benefits from these programs were those who administered the programs and not those who were really in need of it.

Although the number of poor people did decline in America, it is obvious that those temporary reliefs were not designed to end poverty. In actuality many of those programs, especially the home relief (HR) and AFDC, had caused millions of Americans to become dependent on the "system," instead of striving to remedy their own situation. However, although (in my view), these various acts which were passed by the Johnson Administration were goodwill gestures, I do not think that the government, or any subsequent United States government, have done enough or have seen it humanely fit to pass laws to protect some of the most fundamental issues facing blacks in America. For example, one of the most important acts that was passed by the United States Congress in 1965 under the Johnson's Administration was the Voting Rights Act. However, that voting rights act was not a law, it was only an act.

In the year 2007, that 'noble' act will have expired, and the United States Congress will once again convene to decide if black people in America should retain the right to vote. In 1982, former President Ronald Reagan extended the Voting Rights act to another twenty-five years; this will expire in the year 2007. To pass, thirty-eight (38) States must approve this extension. Black people in America are the only group of people who require permission under the United States Constitution to vote. This act should be made a law (perpetual), under the United States Constitution; it is the honorable thing to do. This ugliness and discriminatory practice reflects the *Two Faces of Uncle Sam.*

It is not illegal for government to subsidize the low socio-economic well-being of those citizens who have been historically deprived of equal opportunity in America; but the government should devise the ways and the means by which these citizens can at least adequately provide for themselves without having to depend on "stop-gap measures which are considered to be an economic and financial burden to both the government and tax payers as well.

For example, David Faber in his research cited the number of food stamps recipients in the 1960s as a classical example. Farber stated that "in 1965 only about 633,000 people received what was often minimum aid at a barely noticeable cost of $36 million. A decade later,"[12] (in 1975) "over 17 million people benefited from the food stamps at a cost of $4.3 billion"[13] in addition to other food subsidies.

In 1994, over 27 million people collected food stamps at a cost of almost $22½ billion. Thus the government's approach to eradicate poverty in America did not only fail, but poverty was actually expanded and hence created a new generation of dependents – people who would come to rely on government to provide them with perpetual economic support. There are several different groups of people in America who harbor a 'free sustenance' mentality; they contend that if they can get something for nothing, why bother to work for it.

---

[12] Faber, David *Loc. Cit.*

[13] Faber, David *Loc. Cit.*

One critic of the United States government's policy on public assistance charged that the government reluctance to end welfare for those who are able-bodied has intuitively destroyed the lives of millions of people (minorities), because the allocation of public assistance has actually prevented these people from doing for themselves and to achieve their dreams the way other people do. This critic contended that the government should revamp the welfare program and used the funds to train welfare recipients. He further argued that if there was no welfare, the people who are dependent on it (welfare) for survival "would get by" and find jobs just like others do.

Despite the welfare expansion programs and the Community Action Programs (CAP), which were actually designed to train and prepare the economically down-trodden for future independence and to rid themselves of poverty and ignorance, these people (the minority class) still continue to tarry within the ranks of the poor.

One school of thought which had began to romanticize the economic, social, and cultural revolution of the 1960s has now begun to distrust the system and also begun to lose faith in the American dream for all Americans.

Another school of thought still cherishes high hopes and has faith in the American system in terms of all those who want to pursue their dream to its fullest.

In the book *American Values*, co-authored by David Bender, Bruno Leone, Kenneth Sibler, and Katherine S. Newman (contributing writers) squared off with each other on different views as to whether the American dream is still in focus and reachable, or whether it is obscure and is out of reach for most Americans. Under the captions "Declining Fortunes," Newman contended that the "American dream is now out of reach for millions of Americans ... despite hard work...." that "many baby boomers have found themselves shut out of the American dream."

Sibler, on the other hand, approached the future of America with much more optimism. He contended that "the American dream is still alive," and the "people have more disposable income; that income doubled from 1960 to 1992 and that more Americans report better standard of living than their parents."[14]

Sibler maintained that there is a great decline in interest rates and that "the availability of homes for future home buyers proves that the American dream can be achieved. In the author's view, the American standard of living has not declined; those who feel that it has have failed to take into consideration the large influx of immigrants who came into the United States from other countries and who have placed a tremendous financial and economic strain on the American economic, social, education, health, housing, and delivery system.

One of the fallacies of the American dream in the view of Katherine Newman is that "the dream is out of reach for millions of Americans."[15] But Newman failed to comprehend the fact that Americans on a whole are consuming a great proportion of the world's resources in an effort to maintain a lavish and wanton lifestyle and to sustain a high standard of living over and above that of all other industrial developed nations.

It is not that the standard of living in America is declining; quite the contrary. In my view, the standard is much too high. Many Americans might probably find this argument unsound and without merit, but the fact of the matter is, a rich man in

[14] Bender, David; Bruno, Leone; Sibler, Kenneth; Newman, Katherine S. *American Values*, Greenhaven Press Inc., San Diego, Cal. 1995 p. 66

[15] Bender, David; Bruno, Leone; Sibler, Kenneth; Newman, Katherine S. *Op.Cit.* 138

FACTS OR FALLACY?

another country would probably be classified as a poor man in
United States. For example, the AFDC and food stamps
benefits for a family of six in New York State as of 3/98 was
$1,317.00 per month. This is much more money than what
some people in some other countries earned for a whole year.
It is also much more money than what many civil servants
would earn on a monthly basis in some other countries. To this
end, I find Kenneth Silber's argument (that the American
dream is alive and well) has much more credibility than that of
Katherine Newman.

A young man who came to the United States from the West
Indies in the 1980s and worked as a auto mechanic now
operates his own business. He buys 'crashed cars' at the
auction, fixes them up, and sells them at a profit. When he was
asked if he believes in the American dream, he replied, "I am
a living example of the American dream; but it is hard work. I
started business in my backyard, but today I own and operate a
large garage in a very busy neighborhood. If you come to this
country (referring to America), and you adopt the white man's
work ethic, and work hard, you can achieve anything that you
want. I am not rich, but I am doing ok for myself and my
family. Don't let anybody fool you, this country is not a "bed
of roses," you must work hard if you want to reach anywhere in
life."

The key phase in this statement is "the white man's work
ethic."

Does the white man (in America) adhere to the work ethic
more than other races or people from other countries?

Bender and Leone, in *American Values*, quoting from
Charles Colson and Jack Eckerd, on *Work Ethic in America*,
contended that America has lost its work ethic and that "the
death of work ethic in America is the result of the loss of a

53

spiritual center in our society."[16] And quoting from a former secretary of Health and Human Services, Louis Sullivan, Bender stated that the first department of education is the family." That the "parents need to instill in their children the values of hard work, doing one's best and knowing the value of a hard-earned dollar. If we are to restore the work ethic, we must teach our children that there are virtue and dignity in work. They must learn the important of individual responsibility."[17]

The joint authors alluded to the fact that the church as an institution, can play a vital role in moral education and the work ethic in society as a whole.

Irving Kristal, contributing writer, believes conservatism is good for America. He contended that "it is not possible to motive people to do the right thing and to avoid doing the wrong thing unless people are told from childhood what the right things are and the wrong.[18] He made mention of the newer immigrants who are traditional families who came here, to (America), "and ignore the tempting corrupting incentives."[19]

Interestingly, it is that same motivation (to get ahead), which drove these people to come to America in the first instance.

In my view, I believe that while the church as an institution does have a moral responsibility, and does have a pivotal role

---

[16] Bender, David; Bruno, Leone; Sibler, Kenneth; Newman, Katherine S. *Op. Cit.* p.149

[17] Bender, David; Bruno, Leone; Sibler, Kenneth; Newman, Katherine S. *Loc. Cit.*

[18] Bender, David; Bruno, Leone; Sibler, Kenneth; Newman, Katherine S. *Loc. Cit.*

[19] Bender, David; Bruno, Leone; Sibler, Kenneth; Newman, Katherine S. *Op. Cit.*17

to play in helping to mold the child to take on a more responsible role in society, and to demonstrate morality in their everyday lifestyle, it must be pointed out that the whole society, as an institution, must first create a moral ethical climate for its citizens; a working environment which is worthy of duplicating by the church and by the individual. Thus the child is not the maker of society, but rather, the society should be the maker of the child.

It is true that the church as an institution should manifest itself or exemplify a high ethical, moral standard, so that the members of society could follow suit. But the historical background of the church and the factors which overshadows its deportment, helps to establish a prima facial case that the church as an institution cannot be taken at face value and cannot be trusted to guide its own members, let alone a great number of the members of society to practice moral ethical standard. For example, the church as an institution has historically been a supporter of, and helped to nourish racism and discrimination in the American society, which resulted in the economic and social deprivation of the black race. How then can the church, on a whole, be relied on to carry the torch of morality and ethical conduct for the children to follow?

Morality and ethical conduct (whether it is work ethic or social ethic) should be propagated through the medium of the educational system; that is, society on a whole should set the standard by funneling ethical conduct through the class room – from kindergarten to college. Through this channel America will be able to prepare itself for the twenty-first century.

One critic charged that "America has no morals." It is true that morality and ethical standard differs from society to society and from church to church. But in order to determine what effect these institutions have on members of society, it is best to examine the social and moral developments of those individuals from different societies in relation to the

55

American's experience.

The Rastafarians, for example, place great emphasis upon he moral and ethical standard of society. However, they solemnly believe that "the earth is the Lord's and the fullness thereof; the world and all that dwell therein,"[20] and that the natural resources of the earth should be made available to be used by all mankind. They also believe that all plants and trees were put on this earth by the Creator for the benefit of man, and that government has no jurisdiction in determining the legality or illegality of such herb as marijuana.

The Cockpit church, a religious organization, also upholds the use of this herb as legitimate. Both of these religions regard marijuana (ganja) as a "wisdom weed" which they claim should be utilized for the enhancement of knowledge. How then can the church (as a whole) be trusted to lead, or inspire society, or to uphold moral ethical standards? The church was the breeding ground of racism and capitalism and must not be trusted. However, members of these organizations could find solace in the views of the 17th century philosopher John Locke, who wrote, "The natural liberty of man is to be free from any superior power on earth, and not to be under the will of legislative authority of man, but to have only the law of nature for his rule."[21]

The society as a whole should be the foremost in the line of morality and should thereby create a climate that is fit for ethical standard. But the bigger picture in terms of morality and ethical standards, or the lack of this duality, must be viewed from a broader perspective; that is, how the 'big churches' actually influenced the development of America to what it is

---

[20] *Bible*, Chap. 24, Verse :1

[21] U.S News & World Report, *Black and White in America*, July 22, 1991, p.51 col.2

today in terms of its immorality.

I do not believe that anyone would question the moral decay that exists in America. For centuries inequality and injustice have been allotted to the black race in America; this continues to be so three centuries later although America asserts herself and declare freedom and equality for all people.

Several books were written by noted Southern divines to justify slavery. "Churches and religious leaders pretended to be interested only in the spiritual state of master and slaves without concern for the institutional structures in which...." the slaves "found themselves." How then can the church as an institution be trusted to help free America from injustices? The church, according to Liston Pope in *Millhands and Preachers*, provided an indispensable condition for the revolution of capitalism. [22]

The church was a base of power for and exercised intensive influence and collaboration with the slave masters. The church condoned and supported the institution of slavery, the institution of racism, the institution of segregation, and helped to lay the basic foundation and the ultimate authority in the world's greatest capitalistic system. To put it more succinctly, the church were allies with the oppressors of the black race in America and cannot and must not be trusted.

While some argued that the death of the work ethic in America is the result of the loss of a spiritual center in the society, others contended that America is working harder than ever. However, regardless of how the question of the work ethic is viewed, the whole issue can be summed up into the following four simple terms: (1) individualism, (2) gratification, (3) necessity, and (4) rewards. Each of these four points will be discussed in the following pages.

---

[22] Pope, Liston *Millhands and Preachers*, New haven & London, Yale University Press 1942.- Intro. xxv

Individualism: Individualism in terms of the work ethic in America can best be described as those persons who have the will power and are motivated to get ahead and who show the self-interest through his or her own will-power, no matter what. Whether such motivation is the result of learned behavior or came about as a consequence of the desire to acquire the most out of life, the adherent to ethical standard as it correlates with the work ethic is an individual expression.

Gratification: Gratification in terms of the American work ethic is a source of satisfaction and "pleasure to work."A gentleman who migrated to the United States from Europe in the 1930s when he was a teenager is still working as I script these words of writ (1997). He told me that he has been working as a maintenance engineer at the same company since 1945 – 52 years. In the summer of 1997 when I met this gentleman, he was fixing a broken water pipe in the men's room at the not-for-profit organization where he was employed.

During his coffee-break, we chatted and discussed the politics of the Clinton administration, and the emphasis which was placed on the complexity of public assistance, and the government's effort to change welfare into work-fare. I asked this "noble" man why was he still working after so many years on the job. As if he had expected the question, he quickly replied, "Because I get a lot of satisfaction from working and it has nothing to do with money." Continuing, he said, "Work keeps me fit, and it kept me going. If ten years from now I felt the same way as I feel today, I will still come to work; this is America."

"Why is America so different?" I asked.

"Because in America, the government doesn't stop anyone from working; in fact the government have to sometimes force some people to go out and find a job; work doesn't kill anyone," he said. (Please note that this gentleman is not self-employed. In fact, he work for a not-for-profit organization) as mentioned above.

Necessity: People are compelled to work in America; it has become a necessity, and it is unavoidable. Because of the value which Americans have placed upon material possessions, economic stability and the high standard of living which they crave and strive for, it is essential for one to work consistently in order to maintain that high quality of excellence. In my view, the elements of circumstance in society necessitate working constantly, and America is no exception. Hence the necessity to work, which is exerted by circumstance, is a factor which make it unavoidable for every capable individual to find and secure a job to support his- or herself.

Those who have a taste for the finer things of life (the American dream), such as a house, a big car, consumer goods in abundance, vacation, higher education, and so on, will always devote themselves to hard work in order to achieve these things. Those who have no desire to work and no vision of the future will no doubt violate the code of the work ethic and avoid working for a living.

Rewards: Adherents of the work ethic do so because of the returns or incentives, which they receive as reciprocation, or as compensation for working. High returns for one's labor is an incentive and is a requisite for working. One critic argued that because of low returns and inadequate rewards, a great number of people in America are unable to realize their dreams and as a result they have decided to abstain themselves from the work force and chose, instead, to rely on government subsistence for a living.

Hence the question of adhering to the work ethic as it is applied to Americans is centered around the assertion of one's own will, and also the fundamental principle of the American culture. This is essentially the autonomy that everyone is allowed, at any adult age, without government interference. But the bigger question is, if every able-bodied person in America is obligated to work for a living, uphold good moral conduct, and maintain the work ethic, why is it that so many able-bodied people are dependent on the government for sustenance and are encouraged by the said government to do so?

The answer may very well lie in the economic, racial, and social policies of the society. These policies, which on the surface appeared to be providing for the poor, are in reality are subsidizing the rich at the expense of the poor. These are policies which failed to provide suitable and affordable houses for the homeless, and are reluctant to provide a National Health Policy for the benefit of the poor, the elderly, and the disabled; policies which failed to make economic opportunity available and equal to all Americans. These are policies which failed to provide education and training to the ignorant and the disadvantage, which would enabled them to improve their life's situations. These restricted policies which the legislative branch of the United States government refused to implement are reflected on the nature and on the "Two Faces of Uncle Sam."

From 1965-1966, the late President Lyndon B. Johnson promulgated a war on poverty. His ardent declaration consequently expanded and greatly increased the expenditures for public assistance; that so-called noble act was the beginning of mass dependence on government for sustenance.

It is now more than three decades later, and poverty and ignorance is still at an unacceptable standard in America, and the welfare roll is still relatively too high; so who is the real beneficiary of liberalism in America? Is it the poor, the ignorant, the untrained, and the disadvantaged, or is it those people who did the research, formulate the policies, implement the programs, or administer the training? I am obliged to let the readers draw their own conclusions.

Equality and justice under the banner of liberal democracy has worked only for two classes of people, the upper class and the middle class; in short the white race on a whole, who formulate the policies and implement the programs. The lower classes, namely blacks and other minorities, are left to dangle in economic poverty, injustice, and social disfranchisement.

Bill Clinton came to power on the wings of the liberal democratic movement and proclaimed himself to be a representative of a new breed of democrats. However, he has signed practically every bill that was submitted, passed, and sent to him by the Republican Senate and the Republican Congress. For example, Clinton has signed a Welfare Reform Act which limits the amount of assistance a family should receive and how long such person or persons can remain on welfare. Thus it is clear that the "old-style liberal democratic ideals" have been thrown out the window, at least during the Clinton administration. Do these acts of conservatism make Bill Clinton a Conservative Democrat? Or is it that conservatism is better for America? I am inclined to legitimize Irving Kristal's argument, that conservatism is good for America.

Some sociologists have defended liberalism as an ideally altruistic system for society on a whole. These adherents of liberalism contended that there are millions of people in society (subjects of some societal coercive system, employees, and members of other fraternal organizations) who have no say in the decisions that ultimately affect their lives; and that these people have actually become subservient to these higher ruling bodies. For example, most big corporations or some sovereign power whose sole function is to control and exercise power and authority over their subjects (employees or competitors), usually do so through the medium of some sort of controlling factors, such as "obedience, conformity, subserviency" and/or some forms of trepidation. All these elements tend to affect

61

how people live, move, and exist. Howbeit, I believe that some organization, in order to retain total commitment, or to develop certain trust in their members, must exert certain amount of control over their membership.

On the other hand, some people, whether members, subjects, or employees, require some sort of policy guidelines in which to follow, and therefore look towards a legitimate authority for that guidance.

Some pundits believe that there has been an erosion of democratic ideals in government as well as in big corporations all through the twentieth century, and that this erosion is steadfastly expanding under the auspices of conservatism. But the author of this book adamantly disagrees with these points of views. For example, in my views, liberalism has gone much too far in the American society in many instances, in the name of democracy, and not far enough in the name of conservatism. For example, under the Clinton-Gore Administration, a 'gay' man or a lesbian serving in the military must conceal their homosexuality in order to maintain their military status. In addition, those who wish to serve must also conceal their homosexual behavior if they want to be accepted. The then Administration's policy was a " don't ask, don't tell," position. If you are a lesbian, or are 'gay,' and you are already in the military, it is all right to stay, but to flaunt or to tell anyone about your lifestyle would consequentially cause dismissal. If you are applying, and you tell anyone that you are a homosexual, you will be rejected.

My position is, why not adopt a 'no tolerance' policy and discharge those that are in, and reject those who are desirous of using the military for anything short of military service.

Liberalism has definitely gone too far in America to such an extent that even some States in the Union are now legalizing 'same sex' marriages between homosexuals, and also assigning equal or same rights status as in the case of a heterosexual couple. These unpious rulings by members of the Judiciary are not only blatant, but are also in violation of the laws of God, the laws of nature, and the moral ethics of the broader society as a whole. All these unparalleled acts come about as a result of liberalism.

Ronald Reagan was a true conservative who believed that the federal government was not a philanthropist; that the government had too much responsibility in directing the affairs of members of society; that the government was "too big" and needed to be trimmed. Reagan believed that opportunities should be provided via private enterprise with undue government interference. He believed that the perpetuity of the 'dole' (welfare) was against human dignity, and that creation of economic opportunity was of sound reasoning.

Man on a whole should always strive to enhance his or her potential and/or ability in society in order to take on more responsibility which can be beneficial to his or her fellow men. Liberalism tends to focus more on the immediate individual interest, rather than on the broader needs of the society in a collective manner.

The rapid expansion of the welfare programs in the sixties, under the banner of liberalism, was not an enhancement to the millions of recipients, but rather had retarded their ability to be self-reliant. Aristotle maintained that "laws should be judged by the extent to which they enhanced man's nature as a moral rational social being."[23]

When we study the work ethic of Americans, it is worthwhile to also do a comparative analysis of work ethic and the high moral standard which exist in other societies. For example, in the Third World countries where there is no welfare system, work ethic and morals are very high as

---

[23] U.S. News Report, *Op. Cit.* p. 50

compared to the United States. It is because of this high standard of work ethic and moral obligation to society why millions of foreigners come here (to America) to look for work and to improve their standard of living.

Those who study the problems of ethnicity and ethnic variations in America will no doubt agree that the large immigrants population in the United States have demonstrated over and over again, and have showed the American society what work ethic really is. Their hard work and relentless toiling, day and night (sometimes holding two jobs to "make ends meet") and to provide for immediate families in their respective home-lands have proven beyond a reasonable doubt that America lags far behind in terms of ethical standard, morality, and work ethic.

Thus it is reasonable to assume that the cultural upbringing of individual members of society which includes the importance of "working for a living," be a responsible citizen, be ambitious, and be thrifty, plays a significant role in the arena of work ethic and human morality. It is interesting to note also that although the rewards and the incentives for labor exchange are much greater and attractive in America, the work ethic and moral standards are much lower. I will concede to the fact, however, that because work is hard to find in most of these Third World countries, one of the worker's main incentive is to get a job and thus hold on to it. Holding on to your job, and do it well, is a justification for an employee; to exhibit high ethical standard is the purpose of most employees as well. I will admit though that with the global trend and the ever growing power of Trade Unions and the union's ability to act on the behalf of its workers, the high work ethic and morale are dwindling in the Third World countries and even in the European countries as well, where workers were long considered to have possessed the highest ethical standard in working, high morale, and have been considered hard workers. But one should not be overly surprised if the newcomers to America have subsequently lost some of their high ethical standards, the zest to work hard, or to live up to high moral standard.

Some newcomers have disputed the assumption that America lags behind in terms of the work ethic and moral standard. Those who make this assumption, however, tend to take an individual approach to the problems, rather than viewing the question from a collective point of view. And so the established norms, work habits, and moral values brought to America by the newcomers, coupled with the high rate of remuneration and the old way of doing business, tend to cause some sort of confusion between work obligation and work destitution.

Robert Merton and Robert Nisbit in their research on social problems, have found that "conflict between established habits and values, between old allegiances and new authorities, can sometimes be drastic and difficult." [24]

In the following chapter, I will bring to the attention of the readers of this book how the American democratic system of government tries to deceive the people by portraying itself as the standard-bearer of democracy, when in fact the system is flawed, and does in fact favor the white race over that of other races. This is the deceptive concept of democracy in the American society.

How can the United States of America be made to recognize and serve the interests of all its citizens, black or white? Lenin provided the answer as quoted by Erik Olin Wright in *Class, Crisis and the State*. Lenin stated that "the state is a product and a manifestation of the irreconcilability of class antagonisms ... that the existence of the state proves that class antagonisms are irreconcilable ... that the state is an organ of class rule, an

---

[24] Wright, Erik Olin. *Op. Cit.* p. 195

organ for oppression of one class by another ... The state is a special organization of force: it is an organization of violence for the suppression of another class."[25]

Lenin called for the replacement of Bureaucracy and Parliamentary Representation. He stated that "if the working class wishes to take power and to rule, they must destroy the old capitalistic structures and set up new ones."[26]

But replacing the old bureaucratic system of government and its parliamentary representation with new representatives will not solve the woes of the working class. Not unless, however, the working class can participate in the decision-making process, and also shares in the abundance of the society; then, and only then, can the working poor assume any sort of power and become part of the ruling class. But I do not believe that the United States of America will ever come to grips with the plight of the people of color in this Capitalistic society.

---

[25] Wright, Erik Olin. Op. Cit. p. 195

[26] Wright, Erik Olin, *Op. Cit.* p. 199

CHAPTER FOUR
Democracy Based On Deception

America boasts of having the greatest form of democracy in the western world. Historically, however, America has fashioned and nourished racial discrimination between the black race and the white race. America has refused to create social and economic parity for its people; this form of democracy is based on a deceptive concept that "all men are created equal."

America has been blessed in the abundance of material goods, technological advancement, and political stability, especially since the 1960s; but poverty and ignorance continue to plague certain groups in America despite America's unrestrained financial and economic growth.

The nineteen seventies have brought about a drastic change in America's social, economical, and international policies. The immigration and naturalization services have relaxed their stringent and vigorous policies which allowed millions of people from around the world to come to America in search of higher education, jobs, and to improve their economic situations.

The Vietnam war had finally ended (thanks to Richard M. Nixon), and the last vestige of the surviving American service men and women (black and white) returned home (to America), to face a country which was torn apart, not only by the draft dodgers, the hippies, the moral objectors and the conscientious objectors, but also by racial discrimination and segregation.

The black war veterans who fought side by side with their

white counterparts in Vietnam returned home to find that America was still divided on racial lines, although their mission in Vietnam was to liberate the South Vietnamese people from the aggression and dominance of their northern communist counterpart.

Serving in Vietnam was like a "blessing in disguise" for some of these black veterans who were lucky to have survived the war and had returned home to America. For the first time, many of these young service men and women were able to take advantage of some of the benefits which were originally reserved for whites. Some of these benefits were housing subsidies, education subsidies, tax benefits, open enrollment to schools and colleges, and many more. Many of the veterans (especially those who had no previous skills before they went to Vietnam), came back home well trained and skillful and were able to get meaningful jobs which had been previously denied to them. These jobs they could not have acquired prior to their induction into the military because of the lack of training. Many also took advantage of additional training which became available to them.

But the training programs were being offered by the United States government to those veterans who had rendered service for their country. For the first time, black veterans and white veterans were on par in terms of service rendered and benefits received.

Based on the above narrative, it is fair to assume then that America needs to get involved in more wars in which black people and white people will fight together and die together, in an effort to bridge the social and economic gap and thus unite the races in America. You the readers shall be the judge.

The American society fabricated a system unlike any other system in the world which they called "equal opportunity and justice for all Americans." They take from the poor and support the rich. This system, distressing though it may seem, continues to attract and incite immigrants from all over the world who come to America in the hope of making it 'big' and thus capture the American dream.

Suffice it to say that a handful of the newcomers and also a handful of the native blacks have done well economically, but the millions are still struggling in this land of plenty.

The American democratic system is built on deception; it favors one race over another, and its capitalistic system takes from the poor and gives to the rich; this system cannot continue to exist in America.

In the 1940s, when the automobile industries began to flourish and expand, skilled workers were imported from Europe – England, Germany, Holland, The Ukraine, and from elsewhere; these were the beneficiaries of the American Industrial Revolution.

Blacks were practically excluded from these jobs because they were not trained and they did not have the skills. There were very few black journeymen; many of the technical jobs were controlled by the white establishments and were preserved for white males. This period marked the beginning of upward mobility for America's skilled white labor force.

Incidentally, a great number of blacks did not take advantage of skilled training which was needed and which would have allowed them to get into the steel industry. One critic remarked, "America was so racist that blacks were not even allowed to take the training which would have helped them to be qualified to fill those jobs." As a result, the black Americans were left behind socially, financially, and economically. America had lost a great number of her skilled work force during he last two wars – World War II and the unpopular Vietnam war. As mentioned earlier, America turned to Europe for skilled workers in the 1940s during its industrial expansion period. In the 1960s and 1970s America again turned to other countries for skilled workers.

The skilled work force of America was once again depleted as a result of the Vietnam war; thus America opened its doors and brought in skilled and professional workers from Third World countries, and again from Europe, to fill millions of skilled and professional jobs which became vacant as a result of the rapid technological and industrial expansion which was taking place in America. In both instances, the black Americans were shunned; the opportunity to take advantage of the necessary training that was needed was again partially destroyed, and the focus to meet America's future with a full workforce was again eroded. This laxity on the part of the American government to train and utilize the resources of the millions whom Lyndon Johnson referred to as the "Forgotten Fifth of the Nation"[1] and to prepare them for the future of America was to prove costly to the nations in subsequent years. In the end, a great number of these "forgotten" segments of the population subsequently became a public charge to the federal, state, and local governments.

As mentioned earlier, federal aid to the poor skyrocketed from $36 million in 1965 to over $4.3 billion in 1975. In the same context, the number of welfare recipients increased from 633,000 in 1965 to over 17 million in 1975. Thus the democratization of America has gone much too far in some areas and has not gone far enough in other areas. To allow individuals to live and thrive perpetually off the sustenance of government, thus putting an economic strain on the resources of vital necessity of the society, is an indication that liberalism has "overflowed its banks." This was the American domestic policy under the Johnson Administration.

On the other hand democratization has not gone far enough in that it has not provided substantially adequate education and

---

[1] Faber, David *The Age of Great Dreams*, Hill & Fang – A Division of Faber, Strauss & Girout, NY 1994

training for those who have to rely on government's sustenance in order to survive. In fact democratization has gone too far in that "dependence on government's help has rendered many" people "unwilling or unable to pursue" their American dream, or engage in productive and meaningful role in society.

Aristotle was mindful of the fact that everyone should be financially and economically self-sufficient when he stated, "...how immeasurably greater is the pleasure, when a man feels a thing to be his own...."[2]

Mostly everyone would probably admit that the problems of the disadvantage and the handicaps (especially the economic problems) require some form of government attention and or government interventions. In the author's view, it is a sense of duty on the part of central government to provide for and help ease the economic burden of those in society who need a "boost" to make a start, or to enhance their economic endeavors. How effective is the government's apparatus in dealing with these crucial and problematic circumstances of the poor and needy is open to much debate.

A political science professor who taught at one of the universities I attended once remarked that "the policies of government were made not to work." He stated that "government cannot work effectively," and that "the systematic workings of government were designed for failure." He contended that "if the system were to be perfected, many government agencies would be forced to close their doors and many government employees would be out of a job." But if we suppose that the social and economic systems of government were designed to fail, then we must accept the unpleasant reality that things will never change and that the poor will continued to be poor, and the rich will similarly continued to be rich. Certain segments of the population will continue to be

---

[2] Time, *A New Age Of Capitalism* July 28, 1986

ignorant, and another segment will always be educated. Certain class will continue to be at a disadvantage, and another class will always be advantageous. Hence, the federal government (whether Republicans or Democrats) will continue to allocate a large portion of its economic resources towards the sustenance of the less fortunate class in society. Unless the government adopts a new policy towards the poor and the "forgotten fifth," in providing real and meaningful training, instead of the perpetual distribution of public relief payments, some people's dream will be just another night's delusion.

As mentioned above, it is the responsibility of government to provide for those who are unable to provide for themselves; however, in the same context, it is incumbent upon us humans on a whole to fend and provide for ourselves unless we are physically and mentally unable to do so.

After Adam fell from grace and began to experience the struggle for survival, God declared unto him, "by the sweat of your brow thou shall eat bread." One of the dogmas of Calvinism in terms of moral objectives is that, if man is "to be certain of his state of grace," he must "do the works of him who sent him, as long as it is yet day.... No leisure or enjoyment, but only activity serves to increase the glory of God, according to the definate manifestation of His will." That "loss of time through sociability, idle talk, luxury, even more sleep than is necessary for health, is worthy of absolute moral condemnation."[3]

America, Behold Thyself

Historically, America has always tried to portray herself as the standard-bearer of democracy. She has actually succeeded in convincing some allies that she, alone, can indeed, lay claim to

---

[3] Luis Schneider, *Religion Culture and Society* John Wiley & Sons N.Y. 1964, p.300

this appellation through voluntary contributions, and foreign aid, and that she is actually the philanthropist of the modern world. However, within its own "backyard" and on the doorsteps of the Federal, State, and local governments lies the burden of proof: the struggle of black Americans, racial discrimination, poverty, ignorance, homelessness, sickness, and economic disparity. Given the background of the American society, which is shrouded with racism, what is it then about the United States of America that inspired so many people from so many nations of the world to perceive and have this positive image of America, while so many people within its own borders are blinded and can only discern the negativism and injustice which they have experienced over the years?

There is no definite answer to this question; although we are mindful of the fact that some people are inspired because of the economic opportunities which are so readily available in America. Yet, some people view the country with disdain notwithstanding these available opportunities.

In an effort to establish a measuring rod in which to evaluate the United States (in the eyes of the world), *Time Magazine* solicited the opinions of several notables from around the world; the following are their responses and reactions about Americans.

Kenneth Kaunder, former President of Zambia, in expressing his opinion of Americans, stated, "You have developed your science and technology in an admirable way, but I am not sure that you use the wonderful achievements in this particular field in the interest of man, as God wants us to do. This part of your culture ... if not corrected, could lead to collapse of not only America, but of the entire world civilization as we know it today...."[4] If this set of cultural values

---

[4] To See Ourselves As Others See Us, *Time-American Best*, June 16, 1986, p.53

were to become the order of the day in our world, sooner rather than later we would have a third world war in which no one would survive."[5]

A French writer, Jean-Jacques Servan-Schreiber, criticized the way Americans view themselves as compared to the rest of the world. Servan-Schreiber said that America "faces a crisis in education," that "the level of primary and secondary education is well below the worldwide average."[6] He said that the Americans "take little time and no pleasure in reading," that "they also ignore that there is a world of human beings outside the borders of the United States and they are confident that the U.S. remain number one and unchallengeable."[7]

As stated in a previous chapter, millions of people, Americans as well as foreigners, craved the idea of "the American Dream," to be rich and famous; but an Israeli writer, Amos Oz, epitomized this whole idea in the following. Oz said, "America has promoted and spread all over the world the simple ideal of individual happiness."[8]

Oz was skeptical of how America portrays herself in terms of the emphasis which is placed on individual happiness. He said that throughout history "various religions, civilizations, and ideologies regarded happiness as a collective, rather than an individual experience; but almost all of them are losing ground to that triumphant American vision of private happiness...."[9]

---

[5] Time-American Best, *Loc. Cit*

[6] Time-American Best, *Loc. Cit*

[7] Time-American Best, *Loc. Cit*

[8] Time-American Best, *Loc. Cit*

[9] Time-American Best, *Loc. Cit*

Oz then asked, is this "happiness-oriented village a happy place?"[10] His anti-American answer to this intricate question is that the popular American dream of living happily ever after, while dazzling the world...." is like an "American landscape itself: plentiful, elusive, and forlorn."[11]

In terms of understanding the world at large, in the eyes of the Americans, Carlos Fuentes, a Mexican writer, was very simple and direct; he said, "what America does best is to understand itself, what it does worst is understanding others."[12]

One cannot deny the fact that America has demonstrated and can lay claim to the most stable form of democracy in the western world; so it seems. However, because of this epiphany of democracy, many people have lost sight of the fact that America is grappling with an internal struggle of racial discrimination within the society, in which the country is fast becoming three Americas: one for whites, one for blacks, and one for other minorities.

Even so, Prince Sultan Bin Salman of Saudi Arabia, an Air Force Captain and a crew member of the space shuttle Discovery, admitted that "America's greatest asset is its people."[13] He stated that what attracted him most about Americans is the fact that they (the Americans) are proud of themselves, that they "are extremely ambitious in their quest for excellence."[14]

---

[10] Time-American Best, *Loc. Cit*

[11] Time-American Best, *Loc. Cit*

[12] Time-American Best, *Loc. Cit*

[13] Time-American Best, *Loc. Cit*

[14] Time-American Best, *Loc. Cit*

Akio Morita, a Japanese who is a co-founder of Sony Corporation, is very comfortable in America because of the "frankness and openness" in which people can express themselves and also have "difference of opinion without the danger of destroying friendship." He said that "in America difference of opinion can make friends and can bring people closer together."[15]

As conceited and provocative as Morita's opinion may seem, in my view, if this "open-mindedness and frontier spirit" that he observed about Americans could be employed in the arena of the race relations which is nonexistent among Americans, then the United States could indeed be a 'light unto the pathways' for the rest of the world to follow.

Corazan Aquino, former President of the Philippines, was much more patronizing to the American way of life. She defended the country for the way the system has afforded equal opportunity to all. Aquino said that, "anybody who is usually talented can make it to the top. Social background do not matter, barriers are few."[16]

Aquino claimed that "the American style gives almost everyone a chance to develop his full potential...." and that to her, "such equal opportunity is a recognition of the irate dignity of man and his superiority over the circumstances that surround him."[17] She hoped that the time will come when people elsewhere can be guaranteed the same liberty and opportunity.

Given the extent to which racial injustice and discrimination exist in America, a system which is not kept hidden from the world at large, I believe that democracy in America needs a

---

[15] Time-American Best, *Loc. Cit*

[16] Aquino, Time-American Best *Op. Cit*. p.52

[17] Aquino, Time-American Best, *Loc. Cit.*

comprehensive review.

Everyone who knows of the relationship between the United States of America and the government of the Philippines dating back to the suppressive government of Ferdinand Marcos (who subsequently had to seek refuge in America from the wrath of the people of the Philippines) will no doubt admit that the behavior of the government and people of the Philippines are determined by the will of the United States. Given the close relationship between the United States government and the government of the Phlippines, it is not a wonder that Aquino would make such a patronizing observation.

Practically everyone who is familiar with the social, racial, and economic system in America, knows that the majority of blacks in America are perpetually excluded from accomplishing their American dream, because of the lack of equal opportunity in this country (America), where the economy is in full supply, but where there is a vast economic disparity between blacks and whites.

Blacks are forced to live and raise their children in the ghetto of America; they are forced to do manual work, educate their children in the inferior ghetto public schools, feed their children on hamburgers, french fries, and Kentucky fried chicken, and crave the eating of watermelon. It is not a wonder that white people in America associate the eating of watermelon and fried chicken as a customary tenure, or as if these two delicatessen are akin to the mental capacity of black Americans. Incidentally, this is all that most of them have available to them. Sad to say, but it would appear as if these people are allied by nature to poverty and are probably doomed to be held in subjection to the white power structure. I hope that the time will come when America will recognize all its citizens for who they are, and for what they worth, and also provide equal opportunity on the basis of what you are, without hindrance or barriers, regardless of the color of one's skin, or place of origin.

Janet Morgan, a British journalist, repudiated and simplified the American lifestyle in a nutshell. She said, "Americans are the best at making ice cream."[18] I do not know of anyone who ever disputed this claim.

The American Heritage Dictionary defined democracy as a "government by the people ... social and political equality and respect for the individual within the community ... pertaining to or promoting the interest of the people." Hence, in order for democracy to work, or to function effectively, for the good of the many, the people must be adequately informed and must be involved in the structure of the society. Hence, it is commonplace for the people not only to be involved and to be informed in the functions and the affairs of the government whom they elect, but they must participate in the decision making process of the government, especially when that decision-making process affects their lives and the lives of their children.

America 'spreads her wings' in every crevice and corner of the globe; she prides herself as being the world's largest police force. She meddles in the affairs of the administration of other sovereign states, even when the functions of her own sovereignty are not punctuated by any threat of force from any of these independent sovereign entities.

America uses her 'Open Door' and Foreign Aid policies to entice and intimidate the international world; She supports those who are willing to become her puppets, and punish those who oppose or refuse loyalty to her policies. If a sovereign state objects to, or criticizes the American capitalistic system of government, the critics will be branded as an enemy of the United States. America proclaimed herself to be the libertarian

---

[18] Janet Morgan, Time-American Best *Loc. Cit.*

of the free world; however, she denies equal opportunity, justice, and freedom to all its citizens.

Woodrow Wilson, on entering World War I, declared: "We have come to redeem the world by giving liberty and justice."[19] Ronald Reagan was adamant in applying sanctions to the corrupt white South African regime of P.W. Botha even though his government had been practicing apartheid for decades against the black majority population of this Sovereign state.

The Soviet Union, which Reagan once called "an evil Empire," is now the recipient of millions of dollars in financial aid; yet the American government is opposed to the lifting of sanctions which she applied against the regime of Fidel Castro and the people of Cuba for over forty years. Incidentally, the Soviet Union is an ally of Cuba, and the largest supplier of arms to the Castro regime.

The interpretation of the function of freedom, justice, and democracy in the American social, economic, and political system tends to be interpreted in a very narrow and self-serving way without regard for the rights of others.

A friend of mine remarked that "freedom of expression in America is the fundamental principle upon which its system of government and its society were formed." Suffice it to say that if that freedom of expression is a pretext for the preservation of the status quo, or their own statue of liberty, while denying others within its own borders the right to justice equality and freedom, then America is doomed to both external as well as internal diatribe.

The mass media rival for prime-time, they speculate, insinuate, and create an appetite for sensational rumors and fabrications with no regards for, or knowledge of what is truth, facts, fiction, or hearsay. Yet their destructive manifestation is

---

[19] Bellah, Robert. *Op. Cit* p.35

always defended as if their sentiments are the norms of the society as a whole. Thus, the mass media of America have become, as it were, the controlling factor through which the American democratic system flows. The makers of the news, and the journalistic pundits, are the only human beings that have freedom in America; this, in essence, is 'deceptive democracy' at its fullest.

CHAPTER FIVE
The Lingering Dilemma Of Economic And Social Injustice In America

What does it require for the United States to objectively deal with the whole aspect of injustice in America, in light of the present trend of racial, social, and economic inequality which is so commonplace in the society?

Plato was cognizant of the inequality and injustice in the society when he remarked "It would be well that every man should come to the colony having all things equal."[1] The Berlin wall which had divided East and West Germany was torn down as a result of the instrumentality of the United States of America. There are no actual physical walls in America to be displaced (though there are psychological, social, economical, and racial barriers to cross). But the only walls in America to be torn down are the walls of color, which divide black America and white America. On the other hand, if democracy is to work in America, the whole economic system must be revamped and new methods of economic and wealth distribution be employed.

The United States government must find a way to accommodate those who have been deliberately and forcefully excluded from the vast economic resources of this society;

---

[1] Frederick Ungeheuer, *TIME*, (Special Section) July 28, 1986 p.39 col.1

without a doubt, it cannot be business as usual for America to go into the twenty-first century with this racial baggage on its back. A "changing of the guard" is necessary; the status quo must be revamped, and the economic gap, the social gap, the racial gap, and the opportunity gap must be narrowed until there is no breathing space.

For the past three to four hundred years, black people and other minority people, poor people and disadvantage people, have suffered tremendously in society at the hands of their government and also at the hands of the rich and powerful. If this earth and its inhabitants outlived the twenty-first century, America and the rest of the industrial world will have to drastically alter its economic course in order to make room for those who have been left out of the mainstream of society.

Robert Bellah in his book *The Good Society* blamed the dilemma of America's social and economic problems on "failure of the larger institutions" of government on which "our common life depends."[2] Bellah suggested that "homelessness," for example, "like many other problems, was created by social choices."[3] Bellah and his associates refer to single-room occupancy as an illustration of the failure of America's social policies. Bellah's argument dealt more specifically with the "conversion of single-room occupancy hotels in upscale tourists accommodations"[4] and also government's urban renewal programs which tend to drive up the price of rent while reducing housing for the poor.

As a supplement to Bellah's analysis of homelessness in America, it would be worth the while to examine briefly New

---

[2] Bellah Robert, N.(et al) Knopf, N.Y.1991 p. 4

[3] Bellah, *Loc. Cit.*

[4] Bellah, *Loc. Cit.*

York City's Welfare housing policy. The Human Resources Administration (HRA) will pay hundreds of dollars to hotel owners for single-room occupancy, to house welfare families for a few days, to a few weeks, or even a few months, costing the welfare agencies thousand of dollars on a daily basis (meals separate). When a welfare family comes into a shelter at night and says, " I am homeless," or, "I was burnt out," or, "I was evicted from my apartment," or, "I was staying with a relative, but they threw me out," HRA is obligated to find these people a place to live within 24 hours, especially when young children are involved. However, some of these families will end up staying in the shelter for days, weeks, and sometimes months; especially if it's a large family. More than likely these families will end up in a single-room occupancy hotel where they will sometimes remain for months, costing the City thousands of dollars per week in addition to food and sometimes clothing. At the same time, there are thousands of abandoned apartment buildings around the City which are allowed to rot and which the City cannot acquire and renovate because of stringent federal housing policies.

The main impediments which allegedly hinder the city from renovating some of these buildings are the federal regulations which stipulate that moneys which are appropriated for public assistance cannot be used to provide permanent housing for welfare recipients. Hence, while the hotel owners get richer and richer off welfare dollars, abandoned houses are allowed to rot, and the population of the homeless gets bigger.

It is the opinion of the author that governments are not interested in providing permanent housing accommodation for the poor, but only to maintain the status quo of the welfare population, thus supplementing the owners of the hotels who can provide single-room occupancy for welfare recipients.

Homelessness has become a way of life for some people in New York City. The homeless are everywhere; they are in the subway stations, they are on the trains; they are in the bus terminals; and some can be found in abandoned apartment buildings. Hundreds more can be found all over the City of New York in the armories which have been vacated by the army. These armories are now converted into shelters in order to provide a place of abode for the homeless.

Suffice it to say that some of these people have jobs, but even the dream of owning an apartment seems dim, let alone owning a house and 'a car in the driveway.' But the problem does not end there, because many of these people who reside in the shelters are employed and are willing and able to pay their own rent, but cannot find a suitable decent apartment to live in. If the federal and State government could only relax some of the stringent housing policies, and bureaucratic red tape, and allow the local officials to implement their own housing policies based on the need of the people, I believe that America would be able to solve most of its housing and social problems.

America has grown economically from a small industrial nation to an uncontrollable industrial giant. She has also grown socially as well, but this social growth is concentrated only in the direction of white America while black America lags behind. Bellah was keen to point out that "freedom" in America "still has the old meaning to be left alone ... but in the great society of today, freedom cannot mean simply getting away from other people. Freedom must exist within and be guaranteed by institutions and must include the right to participate in the economic and political decisions that affect our lives...."[5]

Bellah stated that "the great classic criteria of a good society – peace, prosperity, freedom, and justice – all depend today on a new experiment in democracy, a newly extended and enhanced set of democratic institutions ... for ourselves and the

---

[5] Bellah, *Op. Cit.* P.9

generations to come."[6]

I will continue to stress the point made earlier in this book, that many of our social and economic problems require government attention and/or government intervention, and that it is the responsibility of central government to help ease the economic and social burden of the suffering class who need a "boost to start," or who need to activate their economic virtues. If the system of government was designed for failure (according to my former professor) why then are we spending so much time, energy, and money trying to correct a system that was originally designed to fail?

The branch of logical thinking and socio-economical principles must be employed if the administration of government is to effectively deal with the whole aspect of economic and social injustice. A classical example of the ineffectual actions of government to deal with the socio-economic problems of society is the irresponsible and ineffective ways in which the welfare agency deals with welfare abuse in New York City. Everyone who has knowledge of how the welfare system works is aware that there is an impressive amount of abuse within the system. Welfare administrators are also aware of the blatant abuse, but do very little or nothing to guard against it; hence the recipients continue to abuse the system and the government continues to "look the other way." For example, welfare recipients will sometimes use their bi-monthly allocation to purchase drugs, alcoholic beverages, or other non-essential commodities instead of paying the rent and utility bills for their apartments. These kinds of irresponsible behavior by these clients will sometimes go on for months. After months of buildup (both rent and utilities) and the landlord threatens to evict these welfare tenants for non-payments of rent, and the utility company threatens with "turn-

---

[6] Bellah, *Loc.Cit.*

off " notice, these wasteful and irresponsible clients will go back to their particular welfare agencies with the eviction notices and the "turn-off" notices and ask the agencies for extra funds to pay up the arrears. In almost 100% of the time, the request will be granted and each agency will then initiate a ten per cent repayment plan that is taken out of the already meager regular monthly allocation. This "payback" procedure, which is called recoupment, usually lasts for many years. Thus the welfare agencies are actually using their own funds to repay themselves.

Once I reviewed a welfare case and saw where an agency paid out almost $5,000.00 to a big utility company for one of their clients' utility arrears. During the course of the review, I was compelled to inquire of the utility company why it is that a welfare client was allowed to accumulate so much arrears in utility bills. I did not receive a satisfactory response to my inquiry, but the answer was quite clear: the utility company knew that the money would eventually be paid by the welfare agency, so the utility company did not bother to pursue or pressure the tenant into paying the bills; it was okay to let it accumulate to any large sum, because it was 'sure money.'

Sometimes the agencies would issue what they call a "one-shot deal," which means that a lump sum amount would be made out to the client to cover all the arrears; this amount never usually gets paid back. Because of this 'lack' policy by HRA, many of the clients who are aware of how the welfare system works will constantly take advantage of the vulnerability of the welfare department. Interestingly, none of these wasteful irresponsible clients were ever punished for their habitual mismanagement and improper conduct; in fact, they are constantly being rewarded and the behavior pattern continues. As a result, the welfare rolls doubled and the caseworkers' work becomes harder in order to meet their clients' additional demands. Some clients would sell the food stamps for cash in order to get the money to buy drugs or alcohol, thus depriving the children of food.

The question is, if the institution cannot implement proper fiscal and operational integrity and guidelines for the people whom they service to follow, how then can they expect the people to exercise prudence in their economic and social affairs?

An African American male in his 40s remarked, "My mother was never on welfare, and I was the only black person in my high school class. I think government should close the door on some of these social programs and let the people fend for themselves." He criticized the government's approach to the allocation of public assistance. He said that, "the government's welfare policy hampers the development of work ethic among African Americans," that "government should force people (who can work) to go out and work for a living. The same way millions of other Americans do it, including the Johnny-come-lately immigrants population, who do not get welfare, (we) can do it as well. I am tired of hearing my own people saying that the white man discriminates against them."

Although I do not share in all these sentiments, I do believe that government's social programs need to be restructured (especially the public assistance programs).

Almost seventy-five per cent (75%) of all the welfare cases which I reviewed during the years I worked for the New York State Department of Social Services (as a Senior Management Specialist), would have been found to be ineligible (for food stamps, Welfare, and Medicaid) if the welfare agencies were exercising proper fiscal integrity and budgetary responsibility, or adhering to federal budgetary guidelines. Also many of the recipients would have been prosecuted for filing a false application, or supplying false information, or for forged documents, all of which are used for the purpose of collecting public assistance. Many welfare recipients would have been prosecuted for concealing available resources, or for having earned income, if strict budgetary reviews or budgetary practices were followed by the local agencies. Also, if many of our public servants (both in the New York State Department of Social Services and New York City Human Resources Administration – HRA), did not "look the other way," many (thousands) of welfare recipients could or would have been prosecuted for welfare fraud.

Not one client, to the best of my knowledge, has ever been charged with such crimes; crimes which are constantly being committed against the taxpayers. In extreme circumstances some cases would be closed as a result of having been found ineligible for welfare; however, these few closures are only a "drop in the bucket."

I will continue to stress that if our democratic system is to be improved, or even preserved, the players in society (both public servants and also the people whom they service) must take some responsibility for their actions and also for the way in which they do business. Too many of us members of society have come to rely on government subsidies, or government's handout for survival.

The resources of government have been constantly abused. Big corporations mismanage their operating funds and then wait on the government to bail them out of their financial and economic trouble. In the construction industries the big contractors give kick-backs to their cronies and thus triple the cost of a construction project. The banks give huge sums of money to their friends as 'loans,' which they eventually have to write off as 'bad debt;' they then look to the government for extrication. While these games are being played, America is getting weaker economically and the deficit continues to rise.

America is in big trouble and will continue to be in trouble for the foreseeable future, unless a great number of people, rich and poor, high and low, big and small, begin to take some responsibility for their individual actions, get off the backs of government and take their hands out of the pockets of 'Uncle Sam,' in spite of the deceitfulness and deception which is exemplified in the 'Two Faces of Uncle Sam.'

The American economy is getting fragile, government resources are drying up, and the social programs are being consumed at a rapid pace because of the great demands and the burden that we selfishly place on the system.

CHAPTER SIX
The Weakness Of The Parents Entices The Children To Sin

Lawrence M. Mead, in his book *The new Politics of Poverty: The non-working Poor in America*, remarked, "The attitude" of helplessness "can be passed on from one generation to the next " and that "children may feel as helpless as their parents did, even though their chances to succeed are really greater"[1] than that of their parents. But they have failed miserably to succeed because the dependency of the parents have actually supplied the desire of the children and cause them to rebel or feel revulsion.

One of the people that I interviewed for this book (when asked about the American dream), remarked: "To be living in America is a dream fulfilled in itself." What a concise and provocative summation? T.C was an Egyptian; he came to the United States when he was a grown man. He told me that the idea of coming to America, and actually becoming a citizen and living in America, is a fulfillment of his dream in a "nutshell." T.C retired from State government in 2000, he returned to his native land, but died less than a year later – May God bless his soul – he was my good friend. But I will take his remark to a

---

[1] Mead, Lawrence M. *The New Politics of Poverty: The None-working Poor in America* Basic Books: A Subsidiary of Perseus Books 1992, p.144

higher level of precision; that is, to be born in America, as an American, is a bigger dream than just dreaming to come here. In fact, I believe that it is an extraordinary privilege to be an American. This is not to say that everyone from other countries have this craving, compelling desire to come to America to live: because I know of several people who truly don't have any desire to live in America; but this fascinating and impressive image that is being painted and presented abroad of America is sufficient to vacillate one's behavior.

As a small boy in the Caribbean, I too dreamt of coming to America, which will be discussed in Chapter Seven; but the idea of someone else on the other side of the globe, who had cherished the same thoughts, and had the same dream, "to come to America" (and I assume that there are millions more around the world who have similar aspirations), convinces me that there must be a determining factor which captivates people's minds in wanting to come to America.

The question that I would like to ask, however, is; what is it about America that people all over the world crave so earnestly for? The answer, I suppose, lies in the fact that people come to America because they expect to achieve what they could not possibly accomplish in their own country; that is, more economic opportunities for advancements, better-paying jobs, better educational opportunities, higher standard of living, more freedom of choice, freedom of expression, freedom of worship, better and more available healthcare, and bigger and better cars to drive.

I was not surprised when a very good friend of mine who lived, attended college, and worked in America, suddenly packed up and went back home to his country of origin along with his family, at the invitation of that country's then Prime Minister, who subsequently appointed him as head of a major government agency. What astounded me, however, was the fact that when my friend's wife went into labor with their fourth child, about two years later, she flew out of that country in the wee hours of the morning to the United States so that the child could be born on American soil – the couple's three oldest children were born in America prior to their leaving.

The second question that I would like to ask is; if so many people have come here to (America), and have achieved success (and many more are yet to come, and will achieve great success as well), why is it that the black Americans who were born here (in America), are finding it so hard to achieve their "American dream?" There is no doubt that the white Americans have discriminated against the black Americans for centuries (during and after slavery), and that this discrimination which was allowed to fester in the society had actually contrived and formed the fundamental code of conduct for racism. This code of conduct further helps to prolong the struggle and the underachievement of the black Americans. During the slave trade, the geneagram of the black man was drastically disrupted and fragmented. This disruption and fragmentation were further interrupted when the Europeans met in Berlin and concocted to divide the continent of Africa into different segments. But what the Europeans had failed to comprehend at that time, however, was that they were not only dividing the country, but that they were actually dividing the tribes – families – and that by doing so, they were actually changing the geneagram of a great race of people – the black race.

However, three hundred years is a very long time for any group, or race of people to harness this spat of helplessness, which continues to be a stumbling block in the lives of black Americans. We must break the cycle of dependency and unshackle this spat of helplessness.

Mead stated that "blacks function poorly because their parents did, and their parents, a pattern that ultimately goes back to the black experience as a subordinate caste in

America."[2]

Mead alluded to the fact that the black man must unshackle both the economic and the psychological dependency of the white man in order for them to deal with their situations. He pointed out that the black Americans "continued to look to white society for the solution to their problems."[3] In my own views, I do share in the feelings and or interests of the black Americans, in terms of their perpetual struggle for equality and justice, in this capitalistic society; however, Mead's analogy of the black Americans versus the whites, and their socio-economic situation in America, must be viewed from a multifaceted point of view. I will elaborate on only three points, for the sake of clarity.

First, Mead failed to conceive of the fact that the "white man," who controls the means of production, and also the avenues to social and economic prosperity in America, had eternalized their wrathful indignation against the black Americans who were brought to America as slaves, and who retained that status long after the official declaration to end slavery in America. On that account, the master/servant mentality of the white man towards the black man creates a de facto situation between economic success and economic failure. The psychological malfunction through which the white race perceive the black race helps to perpetuate the economic grip which they have on the society and which they continue to possess in America. Hence, the white man with his vast amount of capital investments determines who gets what, and when; therefore, if Mead's analogy that the "attitude of helplessness" on the part of the Back Americans is genetically inherited, then the same argument could be made that the white man's

---

[2] Mead, *Op. Cit.* p.149

[3] Mead, *Loc. Cit.*

"attitude of supremacy" continues as an impediment into the socioeconomic pathway of the black Americans – from generation to generation. The black man must reprogram the geneagram and thus break the cycle of oppression. Instead of doing so, we caved in under the cruel and unjust system of the white oppressors.

Second, I will not, and cannot lay the blame of dependency of the black Americans squarely at the feet of the white man, mainly because I find some credible and substantive indication of economic dependency on a cross-section of a great number of welfare recipients, both blacks and Hispanics. For example, some time ago, the then New York State Department of Social Services conducted a Pilot Project, the intent of which, I believe, was to assess and assist welfare recipients who were willing and able to accept training in order to get off "the system." Appointment letters were sent out to a number of clients, and ten dollars ($10) were promised to each of them as an incentive to come in for the interview. Many were reluctant to come in. As a result, a second letter had to be sent out with great emphasis placed on the $10 incentive, which was used as a means of enticing them to come in for the interview (Interviews were conducted throughout New York City in the five boroughs). As an Auditor, I was privileged to be one of the interviewers who conducted the citywide reviews. The questionnaires were very lengthy and in depth. Some of the questions that were asked were similar to those of the following:

How long have you been on Public Assistance?
Did your mother and/or father ever receive welfare?
Did your grandmother and/or great-grandmother ever receive public assistance?
Do you have other relatives on public assistance? Sisters, brothers, aunts, cousins?

How much would you accept (per hour) if you were offered a job in order to get off welfare?

There were several other personal questions that were asked of the clients in order for the government to get a clear and concise picture of each recipient's situation. Some clients refused to complete the lengthy questionnaire and had to be coaxed into doing so. On the question of "how much were they willing to accept (per hour) if they were offered a job," many of the recipients named amounts much more than they were obviously qualified to demand on the open job market. When asked if there was anything that would prevent them from accepting employment, many stated that they suffer from asthma, or arthritis, and that they were not able to accept any possible employment.

Some of the responses were quite alarming. I did not get to see the final statistical report of the project, but based on the number of interviews that were conducted at my site, and the number of responses that were reviewed, from an empirical point of view, I am obliged to state that at least more than half of those who filled out the questionnaire reported that their parents, as well as their grandparents, were on welfare. Here lies Mead's "dependency theory," and his hypothetical "attitude of helplessness." Mead, however, failed miserably in his analysis of why certain classes of people who are not necessarily of the stock of White Anglo Saxon Protestant, failed to achieve economic success in America. He argued that many of America's poor had their origin in the Third World countries and the people who "initially formed American society came almost entirely from Europe."[4]

Where were you, Professor Lawrence M. Mead, when America was recruiting professional, technical, and skilled

---

[4] Mead, *Op. Cit.* 151

immigrants from all over the world, including the "poor and lowly" Caribbean islands and Latin America, to help to rebuild and to advance America's technology after her involvement in two world wars, the Korean War, and later, the unpopular Vietnam War? That the people of the Third World, and blacks, on a whole, help to build America is not a dispute. But the changing of the geneagram has definitely left a heavy social, economic, and financial burden on the shoulder of the people of color, this resulted in dependency.

Third, welfare recipients believe that they are destined to follow in the pathway of dependency as their parents, and their parents' parents; that is a false concept. We are responsible for our own actions; we must reprogram the geneagram by breaking the cycle of dependency and move on. In order to reprogram, we must work against the tendency of relying on others for sustenance; these tendencies were inherited down the pathway of slavery.

Cultural deprivation is the legacy of the oppressors. Whether the term is applied to a group of people, or a race of people, or a country, poverty, which is being experienced by those countries that are labeled "Third World," is an inheritance which is thrust upon them by the so-called "First World" countries.

Professor Mead should be careful how he interprets the loose term, "Third World." The "Third World" does not mean that the people are poor. It simply means that the GNP of those countries that are called "Third World" is only a fraction of that of the United States as well as that of other well-developed, industrialized nations on a comparative basis. Secondly, Mead's terminology of the phrase "Culture of Poverty," appears to be mere literary jargon. Third World Countries are not akin to poverty as Mead tries to portray. One should not forget that the United States of America and its allies – Britain, France, Spain, Germany, and others as well – have not ceased to plunder these "Third World" Countries and have extracted most of their natural resources which they have turned into finished products and which is resold to these countries at exorbitant prices, thus draining their meager capital. These acts of disloyalty have rendered the people of the "Third World" economically marginal.

Again Professor Mead erred in his analysis of the black Americans and their relationship towards work. Mead implies that the black Americans display a "negative attitude towards work." The black Americans labored from sun up to sun down in the building of America, while Professor Mead was sound asleep. I do believe, however, that they (The black Americans) have a negative attitude towards the wages that they receive for their labor. I strongly believe also that the failure of the black Americans to achieve economic success and prosperity despite government assistance and Affirmative Action programs resulted from the lack of academic achievements, failure to get adequate training for skilled jobs, and their failure to free themselves from the psychological oppression of the white man. As one black American stated (mentioned earlier,) "The African Americans did not take advantage of the educational opportunities post high school period, but believe that they could get ahead without a college education. Later, when the 'West Indians' came in and started to climb the economic ladder, as a result of going back to school and qualifying themselves for better-paying jobs, they (the black Americans) get jealous" when they realize that they were left behind.

I am not implying here that racial discrimination and societal constraints do not play a major role in suppressing the advancement of the black Americans, but suffice it to say that "where there is no vision, the people perish." I do not believe that the black Americans had the vision [then] as to where they had wanted to go – goal-oriented. If the efforts were made much sooner, the achievements would certainly have been greater. This is my inner feeling, and this analogy is based on the strides that blacks are now making in the field of computer technology. I have no statistical information on the number of successful blacks who have done well in this field, but my perception of the vast number of educated blacks who are entering the field of computer technology signalize an encouraging and successful future. This encouraging trend is seen not only in government, but in private industry as well. Many blacks are moving ahead in this field even without a college education. Hence, one cannot dispute the fact that education and training are the keys to economic achievements.

On this account, I must imply that the low socioeconomic status of blacks, the low esteem which they exhibit, the evidence of poverty, and the unequal treatments (by the whites) which they have endured continuously, I believe, are due in part to the lack of education and training as well as the extravagant lifestyle which they flaunt on a whole. I will reiterate, however, that blacks have worked hard all their lives, but they obviously have nothing to show for it, because the remuneration is so low as compared to that of their white counterparts. The people of color in America will continue to be poor unless they are adequately compensated for their labor – this is thievery.

Since the beginning of time, people everywhere have craved economic success in one form or another. The fact that some people succeed within a given environment (good or bad) or within a certain situation, where others fail, (all things being equal) has baffled the social scientists for years without any conclusive findings. Some researchers attribute low achievements to circumstances, which emit from individual cultural background.

In his book *Negrophobia and Reasonable Racism*, Jody David Armour uses the background of a defendant in a criminal case to show that "the impact of background circumstances" can in fact determine the capacity of that individual to choose right from wrong. Amour "weighed the impact of a disadvantage social background on a defendant's criminal behavior in all cases in which the defendant comes from such background. Amour used as an example the ruling of a judge in which the judge (David Bazelon) "propose such a defense"[5] in a 1972 case. Years later the same judge elucidated his opinion in a law review article. According to Amour, the judge's arguments "grew out of his assessment that a number of defendants have suffered the same kinds of cognitive and volitional defects that constitute excuses in cases where mental illness is found, but that they could not meet some of the technical requirements of the definition of legal insanity." The judge concluded "that the mental impairments of the defendant were the product of social, economic, and cultural deprivations, or of racial discrimination, rather than of a clinically defined mental illness."[6] The judge proposed a jury instruction that would permit acquittal where the crime was caused by the defendant's disadvantaged background. That the judge would specifically "instruct the jury to acquit, if it was found that at the time of the offence, the defendant's mental or emotional process, or behavior controls, were impaired to such an extent that he cannot justly be held responsible for his act."[7] If the above should ever come into effect, or be used as a measuring rod to justify the crimes or deviant behaviors of deprived individuals, society would be badly served.

To this end, I am compelled to ask: "Is social deprivation, cultural privation, or economic inequality a justifiable cause for

---

[5] Amour, Jody David. *Negrophobia and Reasonable Racism:* New York University Press N.Y., London 1997 p p 95-97

[6] Amour, *Op. Cit.* 108

[7] Amour, *Loc Cit.*

anyone to indulge in criminal behavior or commit a crime? Is there any concrete proof to support the judge's judgment that a disadvantaged background – social, cultural or economic – is a prerequisite to wrongful behavior? If there is any validity to the judge's viewpoint, why is it that all those people who have emerged from deprived situations and disadvantaged backgrounds (social, cultural, economic, or racial) do not commit crimes? It is widely believed that most crimes are committed in the inner cities where blacks and other minorities reside, and that poor people tend to commit much more (blue collar) crimes that their more affluent counterparts. It is also true that blacks and other minorities in the United States make up a disproportionate share of the jail and prison population. Black elected officials in the New York State Legislature voted against the death penalty because, as they claimed, more blacks and other minorities are on death row in the state than any other race, and that they are more likely to be executed for their crimes than their white counterparts.

Statistics have shown that blacks and other minorities do in fact commit more crimes than whites – more rapes, more murders, more robberies, more assaults, more truancies, and more serious felonies. They are also more likely to drop out of school and are less likely to go to college than whites. However, society on a whole cannot make void the rule of law at the expense of the majority members of society (who are law-abiding) in order to encompass the seemingly culturally, socially, or economically disadvantaged. It must be emphasized that there is no concrete proof that any of the deprivation factors mentioned above are precursors of deviant or criminal behavior. On a whole, government and other responsible members of society and the Clergy as well must devise a way to effectively deal with the woes of society; the feeble, juvenile delinquency, truancy, the criminally insane, and all deprived members of society. Governmental assistance, however, or governmental subsidy, cannot compensate or be substituted for parental responsibility to their children. Parental guidance and parental participation is a useful instrument in the lives of children and is very crucial to proper upbringing.

Jody Amour alluded to the notion that criminal activities or criminal behaviors are the precursor of social, economic, and/or cultural deprivation. If that is so, then I myself must have beaten the odds, since I was also deprived of some of these basic, fundamental things which were necessary to realize a successful adult life. Plainly speaking, I was born poor. But the kind of poverty that I was subjected to (social and economic deprivation) was compounded when I lost my mother, who was my main source of support, at the tender age of ten. To this end, I believe that society will be at peace and will be much served, if we try to examine and correct the effect that a weak environment has on the individual, as well as the criminally oriented – black or white.

Amour seemed to have justified criminal activities among blacks when he used the phrase "behavioral justification" to formulate his point of view, that the "mental impairment" of an individual who commits crimes is the product of social, economic, and cultural deprivation. That supposition is hogwash. If cultural, or social, or economic deprivation predisposes blacks to engage in criminal behavior, why is it that the black criminals usually commit their crimes in the black neighborhoods, against their own people? The white society describes the practice as "black-on-black crime." I was not surprised when I read in the Jamaica Weekly Gleaner of Jan. 17-23, 2002 about a similar situation in Toronto Canada, when "over 300 people attended a memorial" service "for more than 100 black youth killed by other blacks over "[8] a 5-year period. The event, which was organized by the black Action Defense

---

[8] The Daily Gleaner, Jan. 17-23, 2002. p.22, Col. 21.

Committee (B.A.D.C), of Toronto, presented plaques to the grieving mothers of the murdered youths.

It was good that an event of that nature could be held to commemorate the memory of the grieving parents. However, in my view, I believe that it would have been so fitting if the memorabilia were certificates of achievements of the children to their parents. The black family must be awakened out of their slumber and learn how to discipline their children, so that they may grow up in the fear and admonition of God and thus conform to the laws and moral values of society. Unless this is done, a whole generation of black youth will perish before the age of adulthood. If the deprivation factor is the criterion for criminal activities, why murder those who are also the victim of similar circumstance; or why rape those sisters who have lost their virginity as a result of cultural deprivation? Why not direct the criminal acts towards those who are responsible for their life's situation?

Statistics have shown that more crimes are committed in poor neighborhoods by people in those neighborhoods, than in the middle-class or upper-class neighborhoods. What shall we do then? Should the society in which we live resort to the infusion of developmental psychology as a means of stemming this deviant, behavioral misconduct as it relates to blacks in order to cipher their unholy, unpious, and unacceptable criminal exploit? I believe that society would be well served if the social scientists would take the time (through experimentation) to explore and carefully examine the following five points:

Is criminal behavior a learned behavior?
Is it a habit-forming behavior?
Is it a cognitive (conscious mental activity) reaction?
Are there born criminals?
Is the inclination to steal a result of accessibility or need?

103

If we can answer these questions correctly, or can adequately find the solutions to these problems, then we should be able to solve the woes of society. I believe that the crucial fact to the above expression of inquiry has to do with the quality of the human environment in which the "black man" finds himself.

Underdevelopment has perpetually been a major factor in the lives and well-being of the black race – from generation to generation – of which the black Americans are no exception. Incongruously, the black Americans had continuously lived in a social condition that is tantamount to deprivation and underdevelopment; nonetheless, America remains the most developed country in the modern world. And so, because the older generation of black Americans did not take advantage of the education and training opportunities that were available to them, during the developmental stage of the American society, the after effect is that "the parents suck the sour grapes and set the children's teeth on edge." Thus, ignorance, poverty, and the lack of training filters down to the children from generation to generation.

Psychologists have long maintained that behavioral traits in an adult person can usually be traced to occurrences or influences during childhood. More than three hundred years ago, the poet John Milton wrote: "The childhood shows the man; as morning shows the day."

Amour, in his analysis of the problems of blacks in America, in terms of the deprivation factors (mentioned above), quoted from the theory of the psychologist William James, who stated that "any sequence of mental action which has been frequently repeated tends to perpetuate itself … so that we accustomed to think, feel or do what we have been before accustomed to think, feel or do, under like circumstances...."[9]

Patricia C. Devine points out that "automatic processes

---

[9] Amour, Op. Cit. p. 134

involve the unintentional or spontaneous activation of some well-learned set of associations, or responses that have been developed through repeated activation in memory."[10]

Alan Keyes, the black political candidate for the United States presidency in 2000, blamed the deprivation and dependency syndrome of the black Americans on the United States system of government. In his book *Master of the Dreams – The Strength and Betrayal of Black Americans* Keyes stated that the "welfare state liberalism spawned programs and institutions that encouraged many blacks who depended on them to lose touch with...." their "heritage, lose faith in themselves, and to believe...." that "they can accomplish nothing on their own."[11] Alan Keyes alluded to the notion that blacks were holding their own (morally however), "until the imposition of the welfare-state systems," which interfered with their so-called stability. Keyes stated, "the welfare-state system disrupted this...." so-called "social pattern by offering a source of economic and social support ... without any ... pressure to normalize...." this "behavior."[12] He felt that the church and other community-based institutions that were the main source of support for black Americans were also undermined as a result of the imposition of the "welfare-state system."[13] Keyes believed that self-fulfillment and the acquisition of materialism, which became desirable in the 1960s, was also a factor in the disruption and destruction of the black Americans. He insisted

[10] Devine, Patricia C. *Principles of Psychology, Stereotype and Prejudice: Personality and Social Psychology* 1890 p.p. 5, 6

[11] Keyes, Alan. *Master of the Dream – The Strength and Betrayal of Black Americans*, Morrow, N.Y. 1994 p.p 131-132

[12] Keyes, *Loc. Cit.*

[13] Keyes, *Loc. Cit.*

that the "dominant church culture of the black community was the main source of black survival." [14]

Alan Keyes is not the only black American to have criticized the welfare-state system in America, which practically destroyed the will of the black Americans to succeed. Other critics were mentioned earlier in this book. However, Alan Keyes falls short on two frontiers in his effort to appease the underachievement of the black Americans. First, he failed to acknowledge that the church and community-based institutions that were the main sources of black survival were only stop-gap measures, and should not have been taken as a broad-base permanent support system. Hence, it was incumbent upon the black Americans themselves to strive towards economic independence. Second, what sort of "moral stability" is Dr. Keyes referring to? How can any group (or race for that matter) maintain any sort of social or moral stability in the face of adverse poverty? I do believe that the welfare-state system that escalated in the 1960s to assist the poor went much too far in their appropriation expenditure; some of these funds should have been spent in the area of education and training; but the black leaders, the black politicians, and indeed the black church and other black community-based institutions, who no doubt profited from the system, stood idle by and watched until the will to achieve the American dream became an illusion. Keyes criticized Lawrence Mead for castigating the attitudes and behavioral characteristics of the black Americans on a whole, particularly for the failure to achieve economic status long after slavery is abolished.

Over a decade ago, Mead determined that black culture was akin to rock music, "drug dealers, and the ghetto street corner." Over a decade later, the dealing of drugs, gun violence, street crimes, robbery, and rap music is still a part of the black

---

[14] Keyes, *Loc. Cit.*

culture. The black man is in a state of confusion; an identity confusion. The "gangster rap" music, the dancehall slackness, the disrespect for women, the wearing of the "big pants below the drawers waist" has become, as it were, the dominant culture among the black youth of America. The vulgarism and the obscenity which are being displayed in the media and in public places by these "black rappers" is not only repulsive and offensive, but has become "mainstream black American." All these things are the result of the fact that we don't even know who we are, or where we come from. We don't know our names, but we know what we try to be; we try to be like the oppressors, and to look like the oppressors. The "black man" is not destined to be the entertainer of the oppressors, because we are the descendants of kings and queens. The black man cannot be defined by the history of slavery; we can't change who we are, but we can change what we are. For this cause, Plato "suggested a course of action whereby the principles of inheritance of behavior could be used to develop a more ideal society."

Sociologists have long maintained that there were significant differences in the races in terms of behavior, character, and temperament; and that these differences tend to be "predetermined, within certain limits the 'spirit' of one's institutions." It was further determined that these differences are more likely to manifest itself in the art, in law, in literature, in politics, in ethics, and in behavior.[15]

There is no doubt that there are significant differences within the races; however, this difference is much more pronounced among the black race as compared to the white race, or the Chinese race, or the East Indian race. But put aside the differences in the color of the skin; I believe that the

---

[15] *Psychology in The Making – Histories of Selected Research, Problems.* Edited by Alfred A. Koff N.Y. p.146

Negroes do have a peculiar characteristic and behavior pattern, which I believe are actually caused by social constraints, and the physical, emotional, and economic hardships which they have been forced to endure throughout the past three to four centuries. These constraints have created a prima facie situation, which tends to further predetermine the social isolation, economic inequality, as well as cultural deprivation. The history of the black man has been a history of frustration.

We see a history of success, of the propaganda, about the black man, by the white man. How we came from monkeys, how we are "Forest people," how we are less intelligent than they (the whites), how we are not family-oriented, how we possess animalistic behaviors, how we are intrinsically inferior to the white man, how we are dishonest and distrustful, and how we are "born criminals" and many more derogatory remarks. Whatever the geneagrams of the "black man," neither of us can do anything about it, except to deal with it, and move on.

Historically, white anthropologists have created the myth that the white race is superior to the black race and that the black race was less intelligent than the white race. Modern anthropologists (both black and white), have now determined and are convinced that civilization began in Africa and that the black man is the source of knowledge. One social scientist referred to this historical misconception, or myth (mentioned above), as "...the re-emergent tradition of social evolutionism, and pre-anthropological conception of culture ... in order to delineate the major outlines of the late nineteenth-century image of the dark-skinned savage."[16]

Not only have these early researchers created this misconception about the black race, but modern intellectuals

---

[16] Stocking, jr. George W. *Race, Culture and Evolution* University of Chicago Press, Chicago. 1968 p.p 119-120

have now begun to reject the writings of these nineteenth-century writers as less significant. Some of the works of these men, like John Dewey, Thorstein Vebsen, Franz Boas, E.B.Taylor, Franklin Giddens, and many more, who created and propagandized these myths, should be deleted from readable informative materials. But in spite of these negative overtones about the "dark-skinned savage" it was concluded that "reason was the same in all men and equally possessed by all, regardless of the differences of the races."[17]

In his book *Race, Culture, and Evolution*, George W. Stocking, Jr. argued that "during the delicate process of evolution, a multiplicity of human groups developed along lines which moved in general towards the social and cultural forms of western Europe...." and that "along the way, different groups have diverged and regressed, stood still, or even died out...."[18] Continuing, he stated that "the progress of the 'lower races' had been retarded or even stopped." Stocking, Jr. went on to say that "...racial differences ... had caused the lower races to lag behind or to fall by the wayside.... Differences," he said, existed nonetheless, and they were such that only the large-brained, white-skinned races had in fact ascended to the top of the pyramid."[19] These early feebleminded men actually determined that men and apes were one and of the same race – "savage," "barbarous," or "uncivilized." It is interesting to note that these men (mentioned above) who claimed to have studied the existence and descent of man had no knowledge that man was created by and in the image of God, and therefore cannot and should not be equated with apes and baboons, which are

---

[17] Stocking, jr. *Loc. Cit.*

[18] Stocking, jr. *Loc. Cit.*

[19] Stocking, jr. *Loc. Cit.*

among the lower classes of animals.

Genesis Chapter 1: Verse 26, said: "and God said let us make man in our image after our likeness...." Verse 27: "so God created man in his own image...."[20] If the ancestor of man is an ape or a baboon, then obviously God is an ape or baboon; this is ludicrous. So the question of the large-brained white-skinned race, superiority, upper-class, and racial hierarchy as portrayed by these idiotic thinkers should be dismissed by all men of knowledge as sheer madness. But if there is any truth to some of what these eighteenth-century and nineteenth-century anthropologists had said, that "along the way" of development, "different groups had diverged, regressed, stood still, or died out," then it would appear as if the "dark-skinned savages" (as the Negroes were called) are the "strongest link" in this chain of human development; because, clearly, the Negroes have withstood more physical, psychological, social, and economic hardship than any other human race on the earth; and in spite of all the above hardships they are still surviving, and moving forward, upward. But if the white race concocted and subsequently filched the black race out of their birthright, and forced them into being subservient and dependent, then not only should the record be corrected and set straight, on a whole, but the black man should reclaim his rightful place in the society in which he lives, and thus begin to take a leadership role, in the said society, instead of lagging behind, lusting, and blaming everyone else for his woes.

The white man has always lumped the people of African descent together in the same category of race, color, characteristic, behavior, and attitude. But the differences in cultural upbringing among the Negroes in terms of educational achievements, values, behavior pattern, attitudes, and lifestyles

---

[20] *Bible*, Genesis Chap. 1: verses 26,27

have played a very significant role in the lives of the descendants of Africa in terms of success or failure. The differences in cultural upbringing, the failure to achieve economic success and the lack of, or the absence of acceptable values are much more pronounced among the black Americans than most other groups in America. They (the black Americans), seem to lag far behind most other groups or race in America in almost every avenue of success (except in sports). The lack of proper housing and living conditions, the lack of proper education, the failure in to achieve economic success, unacceptable behavior pattern, failure to exhibit good attitude, failure to obtain proper training, lack of discipline, and many more; in all these areas, the black Americans fall below the standard of expectations.

Research has shown that even the "latecomers" from the Caribbean Islands as well as people from other parts of the world (especially the Koreans and the Chinese) are doing much better in the above areas, and are climbing the achievement ladder much faster than the black Americans are.

I have lived in three of the most populated boroughs in New York City: Brooklyn, Bronx, and Queens, before I moved to Nassau county, and subsequently Westchester County. These boroughs are domicile for small businesses: restaurants, barber shops, auto body repair shops, auto mechanic shops, delis, small grocery stores, supermarkets, pharmacies, liquor stores, hardware, and many more. However, I do not know of any of these businesses that are either owned and or operated by a black American person. About 90-95% of these businesses are owned and/or operated by whites, Latinos, Caribbean immigrants, Koreans, or others. However, statistics have shown that at any given time anyone of these businesses are likely to be robbed and or burglarized by a black American male. Some of the things that puzzle me about the black Americans are that, although they were born here (in America), and have lived here for over three hundred years (generation after generation), they still manage to walk different from their white counterparts and different from other people from other countries as well. Their idiomatic way of speaking is also much different from the whites; their eating habits are also much different. Their customary way of eating is typical to that of fried chicken, spare ribs, and watermelon. The whites have used these habit-forming behaviors to stigmatize the black Americans offensively.

I also find that the writings and the expressions of the black Americans are substandard to those of the whites and also fall below standard English on a whole; this I find to be rampant, even among those who are college-educated.

In the book *How to Make Black America Better*, compiled and edited by Travis Smiley, Maxine Waters, a black Congresswoman from the 35th Congressional District in California, expressed her concern about the sorry state of affairs of the black Americans, and proposed her viewpoints on how to make their lives better. After citing all of the things that are wrong and the seemingly injustices that are apportioned to the black Americans, she is inclined to blame their sorry state of affairs on the systematic doings of the American society. Waters' solutions to black problems are that "every home, every barbershop, every beauty shop, more Saturday schools (I suppose she is a seventh day Adventist), every church, every social club – sororities and fraternities – must adopt a plan, to teach, to instill, and to train black people how to love themselves and each other. "Everything," she said, "begins with the belief in self … if government will not sweep our streets, empty our garbage, clean our alleys, we will!"[21]

I must tip my hat to Congresswoman Maxine Walters for

---

[21] Smiley, Travis. *How to Make Black America Better*: Compiled and Edited by: Travis Smiley, Double Day,N.Y. 2001 P.P67-69

elucidating these righteous thoughts to stem the tides of the waywardness of the black Americans; but now that she has done the "talk," let us make an attempt to do the "walk." Waters' idea of how to improve the living standard of the black Americans are very impressive on paper; very convincing when read; but for over three hundred years, individuals before and after the congresswoman have tried to inculcate in the minds of the black Americans that the avenues to success and or high achievement are imbued in the following:

Get a good education.
Learn a skill.
Clean up your neighborhood.
Put out your garbage.
Change your attitude
Respect others and the properties of other people.
Respect yourself.

A change of attitude will no doubt help to enhance the chance of success. Get away from, and stop "hanging out" at the street corners, or at the neighborhood's grocery stores; learn to speak proper English; idioms will not get you anywhere. Get off the crack, cut down on the big trousers, shorten the crotches, cut the dread locks, loosen the plaits; the youths should take out the earrings; the boring of the ears, or the nose, has a negative historical connotation. In addition, resist the peer pressure to engage in wrongful doings, shun the appearance of that which is bad, good will always triumph over evil.

On the suggestion of putting out the garbage, or to clean up the neighborhood, or self-respect, the black Americans rank "dead last," in terms of adhering to these norms. I am not in any way "heaping up coals of fire" on the heads of all black Americans, this would be grossly unfair, because most of the slothfulness of the black Americans is much more pronounced, observable, and concentrated in the urban areas of the major cities of America. I have met some "black folks" in the southern states of America whose lifestyles and ways of living are a source of pride and a model for all Americans – black or white. However, the following examples are mundane to the lifestyle and nonchalant attitude of the black Americans in New York City.

Example #1

In a certain neighborhood in Nassau County, New York, the residents (some of whom had lived in the same block for over 20 years) enjoyed a suburban lifestyle and a mixture of different people – mostly whites, Chinese, Jamaicans, East Indians, Cubans, Guyanese, Columbians, and Haitians. Practically all of these people are white-collar, middle-class workers. A young white couple that lived across the street from my house moved to eastern Long Island. The husband told me that his house was very small (two bedrooms) and that his wife wanted to move before their third child was born. One day, during a casual conversation, I asked him if he had found a buyer for his house. He told me that the house was likely to be purchased by a young woman from Brooklyn, N.Y. Subsequently, the house was sold and a young woman moved in. This young woman was a black American who, I was told, was born and raised in Brooklyn, NY. She was welcome to the neighborhood a few days later, both by myself and a few other neighbors. About a month later, a man moved in with her. The corner lot on which the small but very neat ranch-style single family house was built had well-kept hedges, and well-manicured lawn. In fact, all the homes in the immediate surroundings had well-kept lawns, flower gardens, and neatly trimmed edges. The driveway to the detached garage was always clean and nicely kept; this was the kind of neighborhood where people pick up after their dogs. The young woman had a car when she first moved in the neighborhood, but after about six months, the car was nowhere to be seen. Ironically, she had never used the garage; as a matter of fact, the garage had never been opened since she bought the place. However, in front of this garage are three garbage containers and a recycling bin. These containers are an actual spectacle to the neighborhood. Sometimes bags of garbage would be piled up next to the garbage containers. In fact, the newcomers never used these containers. The grass that grows along the side of the neighbors' fence grows to at least two feet high during the summer months. Summer after summer, for the past three years (prior to the time I moved) the grass had not been cut, neither the edges; the sidewalk is no different. Penny-Savers (a discount booklet) and other neighborhood newspapers which are strewn all over the lawn had not been picked up for months. Her nearest neighbor, an old Jewish man, about seventy-four (74), who walks with a hump back, decided to cut the sidewalk himself after he complained to me that he "could not stomach the sight of it any longer." With a frown on his wrinkled face he said, "If they can't bother to keep up the place, why bother to buy it, it's a shame on the neighborhood."

Prior to the day in question, this same old man and his Jamaican neighbor (both he and his wife are RNs [registered nurses]) decided to cut the sidewalk and also the section adjacent to the old man's fence. It was a bright summer evening; the old man sat on his ass on the sidewalk and used a small hand cutter and cut about two bags of grass and picked up a third bag of garbage from the sidewalk. When he was finished, he was so tired that he sat down on the sidewalk and tied up the bags and leaned them up on the side of the fence, hoping that his neighbor and her live-in mate would at least put them out for the next day's garbage pick-up; but they never did.

The following day, the old Jewish man took up the three bags of garbage and put them out for the day's pick-up. But the most astounding part of this whole scenario was that, while the old man was out there cleaning up and cutting the grass of these two undesirables, the young woman and her mate were inside the house looking through the bathroom window and think not to come out and help with their own garbage. At least two complaints had been made to county officials at the Department of Sanitation. The Department responded with follow-up letters to them, but nothing was done. Telephone calls were made, and the Sanitation Department sent another follow-up letter to them. As a result, the young woman and her live-in partner came out one evening and cleaned up some of the loosed garbage – this was June of 2001. Since then, nothing of significance has been done and no further efforts were made to alleviate the problem; and based on past practice, I do not think anything will be done for the remainder of the year – 2001. Interestingly, the couple was well aware of how the neighbors feel about their slothfulness, they do not use their front entrance to enter their house anymore; they now use the back entrance and they both leave the house and return at odd hours. It must be noted that I sold my house as of this writing, Nov 2001; part of the reason is to get away from that uncompromising situation.

Example #2

A very good friend of mine who owns a two-family house in one of the boroughs of New York City shares his experience with me regarding the attitude and behavioral pattern of the black Americans as it relates to their way of living. One of the apartments in the two-family house, he told me, has four bedrooms, a formal dining room; eat-in kitchen, living room, a back porch, and also a front porch. The apartment is rented to a black American family of six who is receiving a federally subsidized rent (Section 8). The family of six was homeless, and was living in a shelter for the homeless prior to moving into the apartment. My friend and his family had lived in the house for about ten years, prior to the renting of the property.

Shortly after the family moved in, the house began to fall apart. First, it was the kitchen sink; the plumber who cleaned it reported finding a spoon, a fork, tea bags, and various kinds of disposals that do not belong in a kitchen sink. Two weeks later, the same plumber was called in again, this time it was the drain in the bathtub, which had been blocked up for three days. The plumber reported finding an abundance of dog's hair in the drainpipe. During that same month, the plumber was called three more times to remove dog's hair from the drainpipe. When the tenant was confronted, she admitted bathing the dog (a huge animal) in the tub. To further aggravate the situation, the tenant poured acid in the bathtub in an effort to cut away the dog's hair and free up the drain, thus destroying the enamel tub. But the destruction did not stop there; during the ensuing months, the mesh in two of the front windows were broken, and a third one was pushed out and fell to the ground from the second floor where the tenants lives. Within eight months of occupancy, the tiles on the kitchen floor needed replacement; the rubber seals on the refrigerator doors were literally ripped off. Sections of the outer layer of the vinyl sidings on the part frame, part bricks, two-family frame house were peeled off, exposing raw metal. The house that passed a thorough inspection six months earlier by New York City Housing inspectors was now in need of major repairs, which resulted in a three-page violation from the same city inspector who had passed it eight months earlier.

These two examples are only a synopsis of the kinds of vandalism and destruction that a landlord can expect from the average black American, section-eight tenants. This is especially true if the landlord is a "resident Immigrant." The situation is much worse in the city projects where the landlord is the city of New York.

There is no space in this book to contain the sickening wanton acts of the graffiti artists who displayed their distructive "works of art" on public transportation, the subways, the buses, public buildings, park benches, walls, and all other visible places that are reachable. Neither is there any space to contain the malicious break-ins of cars, the smashing of car windows, and other acts of vandalism that occur in the black neighborhoods. My car was broken in to eight times in the same borough; on one such occasion, I saw four black youths sitting in my car trying to start it with the aid of a screwdriver, after they had broken into it and surprisingly found out that it had manual transmission. On a separate occasion two black youths had tried to take off the bumper-guard and the emblem of my European antique Mercedes Benz; this occurred within minutes after I had parked it in front of a New York City College, which is located in a black neighborhood. The list goes on and on. Wake Up! Madam Congresswoman, the black Americans must begin to do for themselves what others have been doing all along. After all, they can only be changed if you take each of the culprits on top of a steep hill, put them into a barrel, and roll them one by one down that steep hill; only then will they wake up and see the light and be better people – It's a cultural thing.

Some people will probably find my writing to be offensive and/or contemptuous; but let's be realistic and face the facts; the facts are that black American youths do have an attitude problem, a behavior problem, and a cultural problem. A friend of mine whose only son was shot and killed by a black American youth, because (as the gunman puts it), he (the dead youth) stared at him too long. My friend had this to say at the wake: "This is just another case of blacks hating other blacks; if my son was killed by a white youth, it would be understandable, but another black youth killed my son for no apparent reason...." His voice trailed off while the tears streamed down his face.

I was robbed by two black youths (in this land of plenty, (where opportunities are available to each and everyone), during my first three weeks in America. That was thirty-five years ago; but the attitude of the black youths has not changed very much since that time; the black youths are still robbing people and not only "other people," but their own kind as well; it has gotten worse since then. So how do we then make black America better, other than putting the devious ones into a barrel and rolling them down a steep hill as suggested above? Three hundred years have passed and the black Americans are still adjusting to the white Americans. They should be setting the example for the white man to follow – dignity, self-respect, self-worth, pride, kindness, and love. We must reprogram and change the geneagram; we must forgive those who have wronged us; we have to forgive those brothers and sisters in Africa who have sold us into slavery. We must forgive the white man who bought and peddled us on the open market like common livestock, or like ground provisions.

Marian Wright Elderman, a contributing writer to *How to make Black America Better*, was very opinionated in her contribution to the black cause when she stated that "we have thrown away or traded so much of our black spiritual heritage for a false sense of economic security and inclusion...."[22] That young people of all races "self-destruct or grow up thinking life is about acquiring rather than sharing...."[23] Where have you been, Ms. Edelman? What do you think the American Dream is all about? What sort of spiritual heritage are we talking about here? Manna certainly does not fall from the heavens anymore;

---

[22] Smiley, *Op.Cit.* p.121

[23] Smiley, *Loc.Cit.*

we have to labor to achieve it. It is not a sin, nor a violation of any religious ordinance for one to acquire material wealth. However, David in the psalms admonished us, "If riches increase set not your heart upon them."[24] Edelman goes on to lavish her readers with depressing statistics about the sorry state of black American children living in the United States. "Every five seconds," she said, "a black public school student is suspended and every forty-six seconds during the school day, a black high school student drops out. Every minute, a black child is arrested and a black baby is born to an unmarried mother. Every three minutes, a black child is born into poverty, every hour a black baby dies. Every four hours, a black child or youth under twenty-one dies from an accident, and every five hours, one is a homicide victim. And every day, a black young person under twenty-five dies from HIV infection and a black child or youth under twenty commits suicide...."[25] What can we do?" she asked. "We must begin by insisting that the promise to leave no child behind means something and we must hold everyone who make this promise accountable."[26] Very enthralling and heart throbbing, but who on earth made these promises to Ms. Wright Elderman? The politicians? Maybe so! In order to get her vote and the votes of her peers! It is interesting to note that nowhere in the article did I find anything that cites the parents (of these unfortunate and pitiful souls who are "lagging behind") as the ones who should take the responsibility and be accountable for the actions and behaviors of their children. Nowhere in the article did Ms. Wright Elderman say that the parents should scold their children for the

---

[24] *Bible*, Psalm 62: verse 10

[25] Smiley, *Op. Cit.* p.122

[26] Smiley, *Loc.Cit.*

wrongs that they do; nowhere in the article did she say that the parents should encourage their children to go to school and get a good education and grow up to be responsible citizens in the society in which they live. Nowhere in the articled did she say that the parents of these black children should encourage them to join a social club, or a youth for progress club (YP) or a youth for Christ group (YC) instead of joining a gang. The question is, who commits the bigger sin, the children or the parents? The bible admonishes us: "train up the child in the way he should go: and when he is old, he will not depart from it." Thus, the parents should be held accountable for their actions and the eventual outcome of their children.

Ms. Wright Elderman has completely missed her target. It is not those who have made the promises (like the political candidates who are plying for your votes) who should be held accountable for the failure of these children; it is the children themselves and their parents, or their guardians, who are responsible for their own actions. There is no doubt that the waywardness and rebelliousness of the black American youths has totally rendered their parents, and even the government, impotent in an effort to effectively deal with their rejection and their resistance to the normative values of the society. Their non-performance in the educational system of the society is not by chance, actually, it is by design; because black people on a whole, by and large, are the most talented in the society, all things being equal. In addition, their non-adaptive attitude towards the cultural and economic aspiration of the American dream and the apparent delinquency towards those who have tried to pursue these objectives is an attestation to their nonchalant attitude and their apparent frustration with the American system of injustice and inequality. I believe that government should begin to initiate policies so that the parents of those children who commit juvenile crimes, or engage in criminal activities, or refuse to go to school, or who participate in delinquent behaviors, be held responsible and should be punished for the "sins" of their children. Thus, the "sins" of the children visit the parents. These policies, I believe, would probably have a tremendous impact on the lives of those children who think that it is "cool" to shoot someone with a gun, or to rape a young woman, or to rob a bank, or a person, or a store.

The black man is in a state of confusion, trying to create an identity for himself, and also trying to achieve his American dream; but we must reprogram and break the cycle of the geneagram, forgive those who have wronged us, and move on. In order to fulfill our dreams and the dreams of the Congresswoman (mentioned above), there must be a resurgence of the black youth of America, a resurgence toward the ideas of self-worth, self-respect, and fulfillment of their dreams. They must develop a perspective that focuses on the preservation of their own lives and the lives of their fellow men.

I call upon you, the black youths of America, to put down the guns and the knives, refrain from violence, seek after that which is comely, that which is good, and that which is becoming – respect. Be a responsible citizen of society; that is the sure way to erase the sins of the past. "My son, hear the instruction of thy father, and forsake not the law of thy mother."[27]

---

[27] *Bible*, Prov. Chap. 1: verse 8

CHAPTER SEVEN
Inequality Based On Procreation

The "self-evident truths," that "all men are created equal...."
and have the right to "life, liberty and property...." and the
pursuit of happiness as exemplified by the Bill of Rights, is a
farce.

Every American knows that this innovative style of metrical
composition is not only a mockery to the black race in
America, but is downright misleading and does cast a gloom
over and impedes the efforts of the majority of blacks' share of
the American dream and other minorities in America to get
ahead or to pursue their share of the American dream.

For over three hundred years, almost one-tenth of the
American population (blacks and other minorities) have been
living with this misleading and misconceived notion that they
have been "created equal" to the other nine-tenths of the
American population, and that they are entitled to, or destined
to have equal freedom and equal property rights under the law.
As if these were not natural rights, the law makers (in their
wisdom) legislated these fundamental principle into the Bill of
Rights, which make it a crime under the law for any person, or
state, to deny, or to deprive anyone of these basic truths.

Clearly, these basic principles have been violated; not only
do individuals violate them, but they are also violated by the
government – federal, State, and local. In spite of these blatant
misdeeds, no one (black or white), has ever seen it fit to call
into question or challenge the United States of America in the

international court of justice for these deliberate misdeeds, falsehoods, deceptions, and for fraudulently employing the term "equality" under the law or for not living up to its creed and the claim of equal rights (social and economic), as it applies to people of color.

For over 300 years, the United States of America has deceived black people of the free world, with its claim of democracy and equal opportunity for all Americans; yet no one has ever tried to probe the merit of these claims. Although it is well known to the world that the policies and practices of American Democracy actually work against the aspirations an advancements of black Americans, the International court of justice has continued to maintained its silence and has allowed these false notions to perpetuate the struggle of black people in America.

I will confess, however, that in spite of the struggle and the unequal treatments of blacks in America, there is always room, and more room, for each individual (black or white) to excel, to compete, and to move ahead, in order to have their American dreams fulfilled. This can be accomplished though, through the process of hard work, education, focus, and shrewd planning.

The principal standard which one places upon oneself is the cornerstone of one's success or failure; that is, if we place high values upon ourselves and work towards these values, the outcome will always be a success; but if we adhere to slothfulness and wishful thinking, without doing for ourselves that which needs to be done, the consequences will be failure.

No one can dispute the hard facts that despite the hypocritical democratic policies of the American society, America is the only country in the world that has "opened its doors" to the world at large, which enabled people of all races to "enter freely," to work for a living, to go to school, to have freedom of worship, freedom of expression, and freedom of movement.

No institution is perfect; America has come a long way in terms of its denial of opportunity and equality to the black race of America. But my own experience in coming to America, and the achievements which I have made, have led me to acknowledge that the American dream is Real, and is Alive, and Well, and should not be taken for granted.

COMING TO AMERICA

The second half of this chapter will be devoted to my childhood knowledge of America, and the eventual fulfillment of my American dream – without hindrance or boundaries. In the small district where I grew up as a small boy, in the Caribbean, several of the young men I knew have traveled to the United States to worked on the farms – they were called "farm workers."

During that time (in the middle to the late 1940s), only young men of impeccable good character, good community standing, good family background, and in good physical condition were considered for the few farm work tickets which had been distributed by the Ministry of Labor to each party Delegate in their respective districts. Several members of my family were particularly fortunate to have received tickets and also managed to have passed the stringent physical examination which was required of them if they were to make the much-coveted trip to the United States to work on the farm lands of America.

Those who were selected and "passed the test" and were chosen to come to America came on contracts. The contracts usually lasted for several months, or for three years, which I believe was the maximum allowed. Some of the hardworking reliable farm workers who returned to the Island after the expiration of their contracts were sometimes "called back" by their employers in the United States to work as an extension to their contracts; thus, some farmers would travel back and forth to the United States for many years. Regardless of the length of time spent in America, when these men returned home (at the end of their contracts) they would look like "newborn men," much more refined, much more dignified, and much more eloquent in their discourse. They looked prosperous, their clothes were different, their shoes were different, everything about them was different. They would spend days, weeks, months, and sometimes years telling stories about their experiences in America both on and off the farm. There were no horror stories, but some of the "farmers" would exaggerate their experiences in order to impress their would-be listeners. Mostly, everyone was eager to hear and learn about "America, the land of the free." From these accounts, one would get the impression that America was all "peach and ice cream," where everyone lives in comfort and enjoyment. Everybody wants to come to America to enjoy the good life.

Four of my immediate family members (from my household) and one extended family member came to America in those days; all of them returned to their native island at the expiration of their contract, except one, Stephen, my youngest uncle. Steve, as he was called, was the first of my five uncles to have come to America as a farm workers. He left the Island when I was only four (4) years old; he never returned. Steve left the farm and "skipped the contract" and went to Chicago, Ill., to live.

Steve would write to his mother (my maternal grandmother) twice per year; but especially during the Christmas season. Each time he wrote, he would always send money for the family, but especially for his mother. A money order for fifty dollars ($50.00) would be split two ways; twenty dollars ($20.00) for his mother and thirty dollars ($30.00) to be divided among his three sisters and his nieces

When I got older (about 7 years old), my grandmother would send me to the post office at least twice per month, to collect the mail. There were two other sons and a grandson who were in different states in America working on the farm; so it was necessary to go to the post office at least two times for the month. But my grandmother came to rely on Stephen (Steve) for her "Christmas letter," because, as she usually said, "I can put my pot on the fire and wait for Christmas to come, because I know that Stephen (Steve) is going to send me money for Christmas."

I was about nine years old when my mother passed away. My father, who had lived a short distance away from my grandmother's house (about a quarter of a mile away) never supported me. In fact, he contended then that I was not his child. It was not until I was about twenty-five (25) year olds that my father confided to one of his brothers that he had made a mistake in not acknowledging that I was his child.

I was raised by my maternal grandmother with the help of my maternal uncles. However, my father did give me three pence when I was a small boy; that was after the death of my mother. I remember vividly; he was coming from the doctor and saw me at one of his sisters' house; he called me, and said, "Boy, take this three pence and buy fish and 'bullah' cake." He probably thought he was going to die because he was sick and was on his way home from the doctor. As I grew older, I would pass my father on the street, but he would walk on one side of the road and I would walk on the other side. He never did speak or say anything to me and I would return the courtesy.

My father passed away in May of 1999 during the time when I was putting the finishing touch on this manuscript. He was about 89 years old when he passed away. He lived a long life but there was hardly any improvement in the relationship between us, although I went to see him in January of 1996 when I visited the Island.

And so it was that every Christmas Steve would send "Christmas money" for his mother. Twice per month, on

Fridays, I would go the post office to collect the mail for my grandmother and had the difficult task of reading the letters over and over until my grandmother could practically recite their contents like a recitation.

My grandmother could not read, and so I had the tedious undertaking of explaining every single word that she did not understand. It was something that Steve wrote in one of his letters to his mother that initially influenced me and gave me the urge of wanting to come to America. In one of his letters he wrote, "Dear Mother, Merry Christmas to all of you down there. How is everybody doing – Mammy, Mum, Cindy, Richard, Terrence, Mum's daughter ... and Mum's little boy (I was the little boy)?" My uncle did not know my name; he left the Island when I was about four years old. After he had asked some other personal questions about his brothers and sisters and about the family house that his father had "willed" to him, he gave some instructions as to how the money he sent should be divided. He would then 'chitchat' a little about what winter was like in the United States; then towards the close of his letter he asked, "Why is it that all those people down there in ... (name of country omitted) are sitting down on their big fat ass; why don't they all get wings and fly to America? I am over here sitting down on money – the dollars...." 'Sitting down on money' was well emphasized and became a diction in my mind for a long time even up to secondary school. During that time, I pledged to myself that when I grew up, I too would come to America to 'sit down on money.' When England 'opened its doors' to her Caribbean colonial subjects in the late 1950s to early 1960s, I showed no interest in going to England. Although a brother, two of my sisters, and a host of other family members went to England, I still refused to go, my heart was "fixed" on coming to America.

After my secondary education, I went to work for the government of my native Island, but I did not lose sight of the fact that my primary objective was to come to America to pursue a higher education and to "sit down on money," like my uncle Steve. After working for the government for about five years, I took a vacation leave of three months and came to America. I arrived in New York City just in time to experience the City's longest train strike, when the subways stopped running for over two weeks. That was my first "real" experience after coming to America. After the expiration of my three months' leave, I requested and received an additional three months leave of absence from my government. Subsequently, I submitted my resignation and decided to reside in the United States in order to pursue a college education.

My first place of abode when I came to America was in the borough of Brooklyn, New York. I lived on Georgia Avenue in the East New York section of Brooklyn. Around the corner, from where I shared a three-bedroom apartment with friends, was the famous Fortunoff store which took up half the block on Livonia Avenue between Pennsylvania and Georgia Avenue.

It was my delight to watch shoppers, who seemingly belonged to the upper social class wandering in and out of the store on weekends (especially on Sundays), where droves of people from all over the City would come to Fortunoff to shop. The store subsequently moved to Long Island when the neighborhood began to deteriorate in the late 1960s or early 1970s.

Pitkin Avenue, which is just a few blocks east of Livonia Avenue, used to be the main shopping extravaganza of the East New York section of Brooklyn, especially on weekends. The newly arrived Caribbean immigrants would "flock" Pitkin Avenue on weekends looking for bargains and indeed there were bargains galore. People would come from all over Brooklyn and Queens on weekend to shop on Pitkin Avenue.

Farther east is Broadway, which served the Bushwick and Bedford Stuyvesant communities. The whole stretch of

Broadway, from Halsey Street to Myrtle Avenue, consisted of major stores and served as another major shopping paradise for the residents of that section of Brooklyn. Today most of Broadway is like a "ghost town;" most of the big businesses have moved out of the neighborhood.

In those days, 1960s to the early 1970s, East New York was basically a mixed neighborhood. South of Pennsylvania Avenue were mostly white. A black youth was killed in the neighborhood during the middle or late 1960s. As I heard it then, the boy was killed because he was black, and the whites were trying to prevent blacks from moving into the neighborhood. There was some racial tension in the neighborhood back then. I was a newcomer to the neighborhood and was unable to comprehend what was going on at the time between the races. Racism and discrimination were a new experience for me; such a system did not exist where I came from, although I will admit that there was a rigid class system; which one is better, only God knows.

I moved from the East New York section of Brooklyn during the latter part of 1968 and resided in the Crown Heights area. Moving from East New York to Crown Heights was like moving from "downtown to uptown." The atmosphere was quite different, and the people were also different.

During the 1960s and up to the middle of the 1970s, the borough was considered the 'port of entry' for Caribbean immigrants who were coming to New York. Most of these newcomers were professional and skilled people; they were considered the most productive of the Caribbean Islands, but they were leaving their homelands to come to America in search of a better life. They were the teachers, the nurses, the dentists, the doctors, the lawyers, the civil servants, the engineers, and the students. Then there were the skilled workers, the artists, the craftsmen (and women), the draftsmen, the auto mechanics, the plumbers, the masons, the electricians, the machinists, the barbers, the beauticians, the seamstresses, the tailors, and also the domestic helpers.

Regardless of which Island they came from, they all shared a common bond that practically linked them together and make them inseparable; namely, they were qualified, they were "West Indians," and they all came to America looking to re-educate themselves, to improve themselves and to fulfill their "American dream." But these newcomers also had something else in common; namely they were courteous, they were disciplined, they were hardworking people, and they were willing to do any kind of work in order to make a living until they could "get on their feet." In the ensuing years, most of these people went back to school, re-educated themselves, and subsequently entered and blended themselves into the American value system, and thus pursued their 'American dream.'

Nathan Glazer and Daniel Patrick Moynihan put it best in their book *Beyond The Melting Pot*, when they said that West Indians were "viewed ... by the native American Negroes as highly distinctive – in accent, dress, custom and religions....[1] Striking difference from the southern negroes was their greater application to business, education, buying homes, and in general, advancing themselves."[2] Glazer and Moynihan also quoted James Weldon Johnson, who said (in 1930) that the West Indians "average high in intelligence and efficiency, there is practically no illiteracy among them, and many have a sound English common school education. They are characteristically sober-minded and have something of a genius for business,

---

[1] Glazer, Nathan and Moynihan, Daniel Patrick; *Beyond The Melting Pot*. The MIT Press, Massachusetts Institute of Technology, Cambridge Mass., 1963 p.33 & 35

[2] Glazer and Moynihan, *Loc. Cit.*

differing almost totally, in these from the average rural Negro of the south."[3]

Both of these writers concluded "that the ethos of the West Indians, in contrast to that of the Southern Negroes, emphasized savings, hard work, investment, and education."[4] It is not a coincidence that the United States of America has emerged to be the most productive and technologically advanced country in the modern world.

The Statue of Liberty, which is situated on Liberty Island in New York, stands erect in its splendor of human concrete structure, and is forever gesticulating (and will continue to do so as long as America exists) with outstretched passive arms, welcoming the 'poor,' the 'needy,' the 'tired,' and the 'feeble,' who come to America from around the world looking for a better life. But the euphemism that is expressed in this orgy of hospitality, which is extended by this graven image of humanity, seemed to have suppressed an hidden agenda of the domestic policy of the United States. Some Americans are critical of the United States' 'open door' immigration policy, and have contended that the influx of foreigners who have come to the United States from other countries are taking away jobs from Americans and are also putting additional burden on the economic and educational system of the country.

On the contrary, the newcomers have become major contributors to the development and advancement of the United States of America in every conceivable aspect of its industrial revolution. In fact, the United States government has actually initiated the recruitment of skilled and professional people from overseas to add to their workforce and to boost their production output. The country also provides additional training for those

[3] Glazer and Moynihan, *Loc. Cit*

[4] Glazer and Moynihan, *Loc. Cit*

newcomers who need it. With this additional training, coupled with the skills and professionalism that these people have brought to America, they (the newcomers) have become productive citizens of America. These new productive resources which some critics saw as an encroachment on their so-called God-given rights to be 'left alone' also help to generate and add to the greatness of the United States of America.

Hence, America is not experiencing any economic, financial, or educational burden as a result of new immigrants, but rather America is reaping an abundance of talents, skills, and professionalism, in addition to the constant revitalization of new sources of revenues from the newcomers. One of the most sophisticated and powerful remedies that a society can ever establish to combat poverty and backwardness is the ability to train its productive forces, both in education, skillfulness, and professionalism. America has satisfactorily been able to outsmart the world and has robbed developing countries of their most cherished resources, their talented citizens.

They (the United States officials) have succeeded in implementing this policy, not only through their 'open door' immigration policies of 'coming to America,' but also through economic opportunities and their open enrollment policies to their elaborate and most advanced educational and technological systems in the world.

By offering educational opportunities and high-paying jobs to these talented newcomers, America has managed to stay on top of the world, economically, financially, technologically, educationally, and healthy. Thus America will remain great as long as her "open door" policy remains in effect.

One of the most effective and powerful antidotes that a society can ever establish to combat poverty and backwardness is the ability to train and educate its productive forces.

In the late 1950s to the middle of the 1960s, England opened its doors to her former colonial subjects of the Caribbean Islands. Many of the Islanders took advantage of this opportunity to make a better life for themselves and their families in England. Most of the then migrants were the rural small farmers and the unskilled who had no meaningful jobs. Some had to sell their plots of land, their few heads of goats or their cows or their few pigs and managed to 'save up' the fare in order to sail on the Begona or the Monsterat which were the most popular and main form of transportation to England.

Incidentally, the majority of those rural immigrants who went to England were forced to retain their peasantry or 'country man/country woman' status, throughout the rest of their lifetime, which they happened to have spent in England – very few went back home to their Islands. Because the British government failed to provide meaningful training to the newcomers, they (the newcomers) were forced to do manual labor and menial work in order to survive. The Caribbean peasants or "country man" or "country woman" as they are popularly called have a peculiar characteristic that bound them together: They walk funny, they talk funny, and they dress funny. Their characteristics could almost be classified as that of a sub-culture, as compared to that of their urban counterparts.

Ironically, people with similar backgrounds who come to America do much better than their British counterparts; not only economically and financially, but also educationally, socially, and technologically. However, I will not lose sight of the fact that the British government has developed the expertise in providing social welfare for these people rather than providing them with training.

While the United States of America was attracting and getting the best of the productive citizens of the Caribbean Islands, the Islands themselves were losing the choicest of their workforce. Caribbean officials referred to this adventure as the 'brain drain.' But the old, the tired, the ignorant, the feeble-minded, the uneducated, and the social misfits were left behind. It is important to note, however, that the majority of those who came eventually sponsored (to America) those old, tired, ignorant, feeble-minded, uneducated, and social misfits whom they had left behind. Most of these new arrivals landed in Brooklyn, New York, and settled in Brooklyn, for a while. Some worked two and three jobs to 'make ends meet;' but after those 'ends were met,' many moved out of the borough to other boroughs or suburban areas to make 'room' for others. And room they did make, because today, parts of Brooklyn, namely East New York, Bedford Stuyvesant, Ocean Hill, and Brownsville, have become a sordid piece of New York City. I would not dare classify all the residents of these neighborhood as part of this sordidness, but some sections of these places have become the 'breeding ground' for crime, obliterated by drug addicts and drug dealers, prostitution, auto body shops, dilapidated and abandoned buildings. These places have become so perilous that even the regular everyday citizens of these communities are afraid to walk these 'mean streets' after dark.

My first ten years in America were spent in Brooklyn. I worked occasionally in and out of the borough during the last twenty-five years before my final exit. However, I would visit the borough once in a while to see old friends and acquaintances. The borough has undergone some major changes during my twenty years' absence. But I will admit that there are great improvements in some of the areas mentioned earlier (East New York, Bedford Stuyvesant, Brownsville, and Ocean Hill), in terms of new houses, expanded business, and so on; but equally, some areas are depressingly squalid.

I took a short walk on Fulton Street between Nostrand Avenue and Bedford Avenue two years ago and had to literally walk in the middle of the street because the sidewalks were overcrowded with street vendors. Farther north on Fulton, at the corner of Franklin Avenue, is another sorry scene of moral decay – drug addicts were seen everywhere; I saw two of them (a young man and a young woman) trying to "brace" up the elevated subway tracks.

I stopped at a coffee shop on Fulton Street to purchase a cup of coffee and had to careen myself among four men and a woman in order to get to the counter to ask for service. Several men and woman were seated in the place, some were having a 'full breakfast,' some were having 'just coffee,' while others were 'just there,' engaged in idle talk. They looked at me with a strange gaze as if I did not belong; I was glad to get out of there. My first few years in America were filled with mixed emotions; anxiety, sadness, happiness, disappointments, and tears (real eye water).

ANXIETY

With no immediate family members in New York (only friends), I was doubtful about my own future in a strange country. Even though I was looking forward to going to college, and to earn a college degree, I developed a sort of apprehension and fear about my own failure (or success for that matter) in America.

SADNESS

Because most of my immediate family was either living in England or was still in my native island, I developed a dull, somber feeling while I became acclimatized to New York life.

DISAPPOINTMENT

I was disappointed, because the picture I had in my mind then about America was nowhere to be found. In fact, it took me about ten years to find and attain contentment and to lay the basic foundation in acquiring my American dream.

TEARS

During these first few years, I was working and living in a substandard environment, unequal to what I was accustomed to in my native land. Incidentally, I did not find America to be the place that my uncle had so vividly spoken about almost two decades earlier. However, I did persevere, and I gradually overcame most of my impediments; as they said in the Islands (when one has to endure great difficulties without any immediate relief in sight), "I grunt, and I bear," and all my disappoints were eventually transformed into renewed hope and some success. My main goal was not actually accomplished; when I was growing up, I dreamed of becoming a criminal lawyer. In fact, I was so set on becoming a lawyer that I used to practice cross-examination on my peers when I was growing up and even when I became an adult. I did not go to law school when I graduated from college, but instead, I attended the Graduate School of the Social Sciences.

Circumstances over which (then) I had no control entangled me; but with better planning, I could have been what I wanted to be, a criminal lawyer, over and over again.

HAPPINESS

Within those first five years, I was accepted and was attending a reputable University in the New York City area. Thus my dream of coming to America to pursue higher education was met with success in my first five years in America. To this end, I must conclude that the American dream is real, and alive, and can be realized by anyone who pursued it. The rest of this story is an historical omen.

CHAPTER EIGHT
Why Blame Others For Your Failures?

Paul Gray, in Time-American Best, punctuated Alexis De Tocqueville's viewpoints of the American society on a whole, and the country's strength and weaknesses as it relates to the problems of black and white in America. In speaking of America, De Tocqueville wrote: "It is still the place among all others where the play of human nature is allowed the greatest latitude, for good and ill. It is still the place that can make itself even better by deciding it to be so."[1]

In this chapter, the author will turn his attention to the existing circumstances of the social and economic status of the majority of African Americans,(and other minorities), using as an example an incident which occurred in the borough of Brooklyn, New York in the winter of 1995. This incident, which was witnessed by the author, illustrated and highlighted the primary focus of this book, that indolence and the lack of motivation tend to impede one's ability to pursue his or her American dream.

Permit me to ask, however, "Is there any truth to the argument which has been put forward by the African Americans, that they, as a group, have been excluded from the opportunities which the American society has to offer?"

As I penned the following paragraph, I am again forced to

---

[1] Gray, Paul *Time-American Best*, June 16,1986, p.100, col. 2

quote the words of Alexis De Tocqueville: "Men will not receive truth from their enemies, and it is very seldom offered to them by their friends."[2]

I do not consider myself an enemy of the black Americans, therefore I have no reason to withhold the truth from them. I will not altogether picture myself to be a friend either; hence, I have no need to conceal the truth. I will adopt an achromatic approach to their problems and try to put forth my views based on my own perspective.

The sky was gray and obscured; but from a distance (at the corner of Bedford and Atlantic Avenues, in Brooklyn, New York), one could see the pinnacle of the Williamsburg Savings Bank on Hanson Place. The clock, embedded in a outermost structure, read 9: 30 a.m., the temperature recorded on its dial read 29° F. Half a block away (between Atlantic Avenue and Pacific Street), was a homeless shelter for men.

It was Valentine's day, February 14, 1996. This was the day when husbands and wives, boyfriends and girlfriends, sweethearts and lovers, and good friends, would share their most passionate moments, by honoring each other with cards, flowers, and chocolate; a symbol of their love for each other – as they said, "Valentine is for lovers."

Those homeless men who had congregated on the block (Bedford Avenue between Atlantic Avenue and pacific Street) had no Valentines; they received no flowers, no cards, and no chocolates, and they gave none. But a van laden with milk and sandwiches would come to the corner on a daily basis to feed the dozens of homeless men who were housed in the shelter.

Halfway up the block on Pacific Street is an Adult Care Facility that provides long-term care to elderly and disabled adults. Next to the adult facility was a crack house. Across the

---

[2] Gray, Paul *Loc. Cit.*

street from the facility is an exit door which leads from the homeless shelter and which is used mostly as an "exit" for the disposal of garbage.

I was on government's assignment at this facility in the summer of 1995. Five days per week (Monday-Friday, for almost eight months), I would go to this facility, and sit in a small office across from this exit door where three garbage Dumpsters nestled on the sidewalk to store the garbage. When I received the assignment to go to this Adult Care Facility, I was warned to "be careful" of the neighborhood. "The neighborhood is very rough," I was told, "you have to dress down," I was admonished. "I know the neighborhood," I commented. "But how long ago have you visited that section of Brooklyn?" I was asked. I admitted that I had not gone to the neighborhood for a long time until that assignment.

I moved from the borough of Brooklyn in 1976. When I left Brooklyn, the building on the northwestern corner of Bedford and Atlantic Avenue housed a division of the United States Army. Today that same building is the dwelling place of homeless men.

My first visit to the facility was on Valentine's day February 14, 1995. Coming from Nassau County, I parked my car in Queens and took the subway because I was not sure if I could get a parking space close to the facility. As I alighted from the "A" train at Fulton and Nostrand Avenue, the change and the deterioration of that section of Brooklyn startled me. One of the first changes that I observed was that the sidewalk of Fulton Street was transformed into a market place. I fought my way to Bedford Avenue and Franklin Avenue, where I saw young men and young women roaming the streets in droves; there were two police cars parked on the corners keeping watch. As I walked east on Bedford Avenue towards Atlantic Avenue, I suddenly realized why I was pre-warned about the neighborhood.

141

As the lights changed from green to red, at the corner of Bedford and Atlantic Avenues, a group of men converged on two cars and began cleaning the windshields of the cars even when the drivers were protesting by shaking their heads and waving their hands in a gesture to say, "No, don't." As I walked along Bedford Avenue, I observed another group of men (at least six to a group) standing at the corner of Pacific Street and Bedford Avenue. Some were shouting, while others were talking in low tones but incoherently. Their clothing was stained with dirt. Across the street at the northwestern corner of Pacific Street one member of the group was breaking into a white Toyota Camry which was parked at the curb. As I approached, he hurriedly put his breaking tools on the ground (a piece of iron pipe and a screw driver which he had used to pry the door open), and pretended as if he was cleaning the car, with a piece of dirty rag.

As I walked by, he straightened up and stared at me in askance. I stared back at him suspiciously. At first I thought he was going to attack me, but he continued to wipe the car with the piece of dirty rag and in the process eagerly looked up and down the streets. It occurred to me then that he was trying to accomplish his task before the owner of the car returned. He glanced on the piece of pipe on the ground and then he looked at me again. I became a little nervous, but I was not scared. Much to my surprise, he asked, "Am I doing something wrong?" The question caught me off guard, but in my astonishment I returned the question, "Are you doing something wrong!" He straightened up a little and remarked in a low tone of voice, "I am not doing anything that is wrong, but the only person that I am afraid of is the police; I don't like the police." I was now in a state of tranquility and managed to ask; "If you are not doing anything wrong, why then are you afraid of the police?" He was still rubbing the car window in a jittery manner; he looked uneasy as he stared at the piece of pipe on the ground and simultaneously looked up and down the street.

I sensed that he was eager for me to leave, so he could finish the job of vandalizing the car. As I walked away, I said to him, "Think about what you are doing." He nodded his head audaciously and said, "Okay, man, take it easy."

Half a block up the street was the Adult Facility where I was assigned for the next eight to nine months. I arrived early in order to conduct an entrance conference with the facility staff. After the entrance conference, I was ushered into a small office where I would remain for the duration of my assignment. The view was great, I could see almost half of the block on Pacific Street. But the first thing that I noticed across the street was the side exit/entrance to the old armory building, which was now converted into a homeless shelter.

On the sidewalk, adjacent to the exit/entrance, were piles of garbage strewn all over the sidewalk. Nearby were four or five Dumpsters sitting at the curb, these were also overflowing with garbage. There was garbage on both sides of the exit/entrance door, some were bagged garbage and some were scattered on the sidewalk and spilled onto the street. I was literally spellbound, not only because of the "garbage dump," but also because such conditions existed in front of an Adult Care Facility. It did not take me very long to realize that the piles of garbage, both in and out of the Dumpster, were not just accidents, but were actually the deliberate doings of those who were in charge of the garbage disposal.

As the day progressed, and the temperature began to rise, the main event began to unfold. Human vultures began to congregate on the sidewalk within the area of the garbage. As I watched with anticipation, these human vultures began to open the bagged garbage, emptying each of them on the sidewalk and searching assiduously, scattering and littering the sidewalk and the gutters with the garbage. When all the bags on the sidewalk were emptied and rummaged, they would pull down others from the Dumpsters, empty the contents, and begin to rummage through them. The process went on day after day for the duration of my assignment, the whole episode appeared as if it was a ritual.

These "human vultures" were young women and young men in their early and late twenties. There were two older women about thirty-five years of age. There might have been about eight of them altogether, but the majority of them were young women.

As I looked and observed the public activity of these people, my perception of the whole *epeisodion* was that of a bunch of "human scavengers" who were there to "clean up" after the garbage had been disposed of. In my bewilderment, I took a deep breath and exhaled with the same quickness; then I said out loud, "Oh my God, what is going on out there?"

A member of the staff facility who was in the office with me at the time, also observed the scene and gave a hearty laugh. Since I was unaccustomed to the street life of Brooklyn in regards to crack users, it was difficult for me to comprehend all that was taking place at the time. I stood at the window, staring, unable to understand what was going on. I was thus forced to repeat my question to the staff members; "What is it that is going on out there?" I asked.

The staff member turned to me and asked, "You know what they are looking for, right?"

I replied, "No, I don't."

He said, "crack."

I said, "What?"

He said, "Crack; this is a daily routine around here; watch closely and you will see what I am talking about; as soon as they find a little piece, you will see that they all huddled into a corner and light it up and they will all take a "draw" from it."

I watched as the rummaging continued and wondered how such behaviors could be tolerated in New York City, in the borough of Brooklyn, under the "watchful eyes of the police." I stood at the window, and I began to jot down notes relative to what I saw. As I watched, and wondered, I saw one of the older women (who had apparently found a piece of crack) hold up her hand in the air, gesticulating happily. Soon after, about four or five members of the group gathered into a corner at the side of the building and lit a match. I could not see exactly what was it that they had lighted, but whatever it was, it was passed from one member to another, with each one taking a puff and passed it on to the next person, until it was consumed. During the process, more garbage bags were pulled down from the Dumpster and the rummaging would resume. Later, someone must have found a sizable piece of crack, because the reaction from the group reflected some excitement and fun; the cold temperature did not seem to have bothered them.

As I observed the group and the passing of crack from one to the other, I could detect that there was a sense of unity and togetherness among the group. There seemed to be a great deal of cohesiveness among the group, each of whom were pursuing the same objectives – to find a piece of crack which had been discarded by those who were most able to do so; and when it was found, they all shared and enjoyed it equally.

Because of my civic duty, and also to the New York State Department of Social Services, by whom I was employed, I was compelled to complain to the facility director and suggested that something should be done to alleviate the problems through the process of a timely removal of the garbage, and that steps should be taken to create a more suitable environment for the elderly residents who were living out their lives at the nearby facility.

My suggestion was acted upon; three days later a sanitation truck laden with crewmembers including an inspector were dispatched to the scene to inspect and remove the garbage. After this initial removal was completed, another sanitation truck with special equipment was sent to the scene to empty the Dumpsters. The following day, there was no garbage on the sidewalk, but those people who rummaged were seen around the Dumpsters waiting for the night's accumulation to be disposed of.

About 9:45 a.m., the exit door leading from the shelter was opened and the first pile of garbage from the previous night's accumulation was dumped; the rummaging resumed immediately thereafter and continued until about 11:30 a.m.; however, there were fewer people. I suspected that because there was less garbage to be rummaged, most of the regulars stayed away, although many of them were seen "hanging out" around the immediate area of the exit door of the shelter in anticipation of another pile of garbage to be dumped.

This scenery of human extravaganza fascinated me, to the point that I neglected my own assignment in order to make notes of all the events as they unfolded. Every fifteen or so minutes, I would glance out the window to observe what was going on around the garbage Dumpsters; I would then jot down notes for my anticipated manuscript.

Sometimes the people would find pieces of old and discarded garments – a blouse, a skirt, an old shirt, a belt, or an old pair of pants – which they would hold up in the air to examine and to determine if their findings were suitable for wearing. If and when they were satisfied that their findings were wearable, they would stuff these items into plastic bags and lay them on the sidewalk to be taken home later.

On some days a police car or two would be parked in the area; sometimes they were seen cruising the neighborhood to observe what was going on, though no arrest was ever made. When the police were around, no "human scavengers" were seen in the immediate areas of the facility or the Dumpsters, but the would-be rummagers would walk on the other side of the street observing the movements of the police and counting the

146

minutes until they were gone. These acts of human behavior would continue day after day, "rain, snow, or shine."

Since the drug known as "crack" was invented, a great number of people, especially in the black and Hispanic neighborhoods, have turned to the taking of drugs as an escape route and a manifestation of deviant behavior. This self-expression usually resulted in committing acts of serious crimes either against individuals or against society on a whole. But the taking of hard drugs is not only a manifestation of criminal behavior, but also an expression of the struggle against society as a whole. One crack addict expressed himself in the following manner: "My addiction," he said, "is the result of the insensitive and brutal exploitation of my rights to get a decent job; my rights to a better standard of living and a piece of the great economic pie of America." He said that he blamed his addiction to drugs on "the administration of the white establishments."

Suffice it to say that because of this blatant exploitation of the right to decent jobs and decent housing, many of these people have actually lost their self-esteem during the struggle to get ahead. Whatever desire they had to achieve their portion of the American dream has been washed away during the process of these strenuous efforts.

I will confess, however, that the American dream can only be achieved through the process of hard work, motivation, and the determination to get ahead; but one should first cultivate high standards upon which to build his or her future in order to be successful. This principal standard (high or low) is the cornerstone of success or failure.

In the eyes of millions of people all over the world, and especially outside of America, the very name "The United States of America" is synonymous to high achievements and high standards in its entirety. That America is an acronym to success is the picture that has been painted of the United Stated by other countries. However, when one gets to America, the scenery is quite different from the original concepts.

As a foreign-born citizen of the United States, I was quite appalled when I observed the behavior of these human beings, who were simply acting like vultures in a garbage dump. It was then that I discovered that America is not really the kind of place that my uncle had described so emphatically over four decades ago; maybe it was then, but it is not so now. The question that comes to my mind is, "Has the value system of America changed? Is this a new lifestyle? Are these behavior patterns an expression of the frustration and suffering which people of color have experienced throughout their lives in this white society of plenty?" Or are these isolated cases which do not affect the broader society and should be ignored?

The life history of black people in this country (America) has been one of economic deprivation, social struggle, mental frustration, and the lack of racial integration. These problems which oftentimes result in criminal behavior and deviancy (especially in the area of taking drugs) can be linked to the fundamental displacement of the American social structure and its institutionalized racism. There is no doubt that these basic problems have a direct correlation with the institutional policies of the American government.

The American social system has undergone an abundance of social change during the past three to four decades, especially since the Vietnam War. These changes have had a great effect upon the lives of its citizens. Millions of American youths (both black and white), in their efforts to protest against the institution of the American government and its unjust economic and social policies, have dislocated themselves from the established norms and have turned to the taking of illegal drugs, and the wearing of long hair and the sensual indulgence of premarital sex; thus emerged in America a new subculture such as never had been seen before. As a result, the social outcast, the economically disadvantaged, the social misfits, the uneducated, the unemployed, and even some of the rich and affluent who have rejected the system, found solace in these wanton behavior patterns. How be it, it is the responsibility of the society in which the change is taking place to make provisions to accommodate such change in order to maintain its identity. The government has neglected to act effectively, or to put a mechanism in place to deal with the cultural changes as they were unfolding. As one societal misfit remarked, "I take drugs as a means of getting high, and eventually, I wash my troubles away."

Because the American government did not act immediately, or make the provision to deal effectively with the impending change within the society, drug addictions among its citizens have literally taken a solid grip on the American society, both in the inner cities and also in the affluent suburban communities.

But the social and economic conditions of blacks in America can be viewed in a broader sense of the term; that is, there is a psychological effect that the economic conditions have had on the black population of America.

Herbert A. Bloch & Melvin Prince in *Social Crisis and Deviance: Theoretical Foundations* contended that "human existence is said to be dependent upon the capacity of the organization to respond to features of the environment."[3]

Bloch and Prince further contend that, "as social change occurs, it alters the structures of the groups...." which is "...affected, causing some individuals to lose or modify their status...." while others "...enhance their positions."[4]

---

[3] Bloch, Herbert A. *Social crisis and deviance theoretical foundation.* Random House New York, 1967 p.18

[4] Bloch, Herbert. *Loc. Ci t.*

They further state that "rapid and pervasive change" resulted from the "incapacity or unwillingness of individuals and groups to adopt to the conditions of change."[5] This "incapacity," they concluded, "may be either psychological or physical."[6]

Social conditions in America and the economic factors within the society have had a direct effect upon the lives and behavior pattern of "black Americans." The deprivation of equal opportunities, the lack of proper education, inadequate training, and the absence of the "right skills" have contributed not only to the low socio-economic condition of blacks in America, but also to low self-esteem and the lack of motivation to high achievements.

Those who have adapted themselves to the changes within the economy in terms of preparing themselves to meet the booming technological advancement of America have become successful; but those who succumb to the pressure of being black and blaming the society for their misfortune have not only failed, but they have adapted themselves to different conditions, more often than not, taking illegal drugs and thus created a new form of lifestyle and a new subculture – drug addicts.

In the words of Anthony Klco, "The haves and the have nots can be traced back to the dids and the did nots." If you failed to attain your objectives in life, or were unable to fulfill your "American dream," will you be able to say with all sincerity that you did all that you possibly could in order to attain those objectives or fulfill that 'dream'?

Our future in society is dependent on the things that we do and the decisions that we make during the process of our adult lives. To this end I am compelled to rephrase and paraphrase

---

[5] Bloch, Herbert. *Loc. Cit.*

[6] Bloch, Herbert. *Loc. Cit.*

De Tocqueville's viewpoint of the American society, as mentioned in the beginning of this chapter. That is, I believe that black Americans can make themselves better, or even worse, "by deciding it to be so." The American dream is not an illusion, it is real; I am a living example of that dream.

CHAPTER NINE
The Epilogue –
Eleven Possible Steps To Your Dream

In this book I have alluded to the notion that the euphemistic expression known as "the American Dream" is alive and well, and is not dead, or elusive as some pessimists or underachievers might have tried to convey.

In Chapter One, I have also tried to define what is commonly called "the American Dream," and how Americans in general feel about themselves and the abundance of opportunities which the society on a whole, has provided for them. I have tried to show also that, although some people find "the American Dream" to be real and reachable in terms of economic gains, financial holdings, or fame, many others are unable to realize this so-called 'dream' and tend to view it as a nightmare which has eluded them throughout their adult lives. While some people have argued that "the American Dream" is real and attainable, many others have contended that for them the dream does not exist.

In this book, I have attempted to show that economic success, or economic failures, high achievements, or low achievements, are not fixed positions and cannot be adequately measured with a yardstick, but are the derivatives of certain fundamental criterion and an indisputable set of rules and guidelines that should be followed if one's objective is to be accomplished.

In Chapter Two, an effort was made to determine whether

people in general believe in "the American Dream" and the prospect of ever achieving it. I have randomly selected a cross section of people from various backgrounds, some of whom were born in the United States and some of whom were born in a foreign country, but came to America in search of their "American dream."

While some believe that "the American Dream" is achievable with 'hard work,' others were not so sure and did express some pessimism about its attainability. Many of those people who expressed this pessimism towards "the American Dream" said that racism in America is a big factor in their underachievements. Some people did not even know what "the American Dream" is.

Chapter Three purports that although America has surged ahead economically over and beyond all other industrial nations, and has enjoyed overwhelming economic growth in abundance, poverty, ignorance, injustice, and discrimination continue to plague the society; that despite great expansion in the anti-poverty programs in addition to some government assistance, the economic future appears very dim for many Americans.

In two opposing viewpoints, some have argued that "the American Dream" is practically dead, and is out of reach for most Americans. Others have disputed these claims, however, and have argued that the 'dream' is alive and well and that most people are much better off today than they were two or three decades ago.

In Chapter Four I referred to the economic and technological advancement of the United States and concluded that, in spite of these improvements, inequality and economic disparity continue to expand among the people of color.

It must be emphasized, however, that although some economic progress has been made, millions of older Americans (black and white) have no knowledge as to what the 'American dream' is all about. The point was made that the American democratic system which they (the Americans) boast about so passionately and which they claim is a model and a standard-bearer for the rest of the world to follow is certainly flawed and does in fact favor one race over another – the white race over the people of color; this is the in-built deception of the American Democracy.

The author invites America to "behold thyself," and to revamp its old social and economic policies so that all people within its borders may enjoy its economic prosperity, and thus realize their "American dream." I am mindful of the fact, however, that in spite of the illimitable economic inequality, injustice, and racial discrimination that exist in America, the positive, boundless opportunities that are available to the American people do in fact outweigh the negatives. But the positives, or the good things about America, do not make void the room for social, racial, and economic improvement within the society.

In Chapter Five, great emphasis was placed on the fundamental truth that America must find a way to deal with and accommodate those who are perpetually kept out of the main stream of America's ever expanding economic prosperity, and that the dividing walls of inequality and injustice must be torn down to the ground, in order to make room for the future generation of this great nation – America.

That homelessness impairs the normal functioning of the human race, and must be dealt with in a viable and meaningful way, in the form of providing permanent, affordable housing; that although the burden of inequality and injustice rests upon the shoulders of the federal government, government alone cannot solve neither the economic, the social, nor the racial problems that exist within the society. The point was also made that private industries must participate and play an active role in helping to solve the woes of society. That individual members of society must assume some responsibility for their own actions and behaviors and do their part in helping to revitalize this impending process. That the church must take an active and more aggressive part in helping to deal with these problems, considering the fact that originally the church played a crucial role and helped lay the foundation of capitalism, which is the root of this economic inequality. That a certain amount of trust is needed between the people and their government if this revitalization process is to come about.

In Chapter Six, I have determined that to be born into a particular lineage is a predetermination to economic inequality, injustice, discrimination, and servility. I pointed out that individual self-esteem and self-determination are a cornerstone to economic success. I have also underlined my own individual small achievements which were intuitively mapped out since I was a youth in one of the Caribbean Islands. A short biography of the author will help the reader to comprehend and digest what it means to be ambitious, and to understand that even in the presence of grave adversities, one can achieve their objectives through perseverance and "a little luck."

I have identified eleven (11) set of rules, which are highlighted in figure 1 – *The Flowchart To High Achievements*. These eleven sets of rules are further discussed in the succeeding pages.

THE FLOWCHART TO HIGH ACHIEVEMENTS

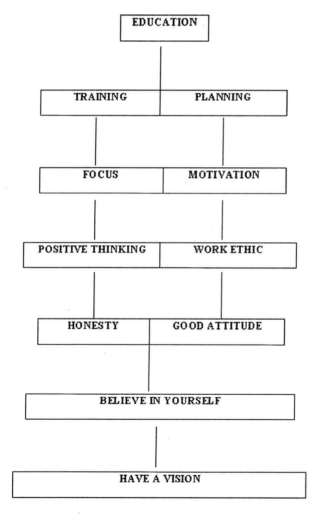

EDUCATION

TRAINING | PLANNING

FOCUS | MOTIVATION

POSITIVE THINKING | WORK ETHIC

HONESTY | GOOD ATTITUDE

BELIEVE IN YOURSELF

HAVE A VISION

(a) EDUCATION

Rene Descartes, the notable French philosopher, characterized man's potential when he stated: "It is not enough to have a good mind; rather, the main thing is to apply it well." One should not allow their mental faculty or any form of secondary handicap (such as race, color, place or origin, or class) to dictate their potential for high achievements. In order to be successful, learning must be a high priority in your field of education. Formal or classroom education is essential for high achievements; but it is not enough to get you ahead. Get hands-on experience; take advantage of departmental training programs. If you work in an environment where training is not available, do it on your own. Good jobs demand skills and training; seek out the trade schools and colleges which offer "adult education training programs." It must be stressed that blacks and other minorities must educate themselves, or train twice as hard as the white person in order to obtain higher-paying jobs, or to advance themselves into higher occupations. Much emphasis, however, must be placed on getting a college education; but for those who cannot cope with or manage college work, or a college-oriented environment, the vocational training schools must be the next in order.

(b) TRAINING

Over the past few decades we have seen that the majority of blacks (especially black men) are engaged in various types of menial, low-paying, and unskilled jobs – watchmen, building superintendents, security guards, kitchen helpers, and many more. A few were fortunate to own dry cleaners, barber shops, and beauty shops.

The American blacks had no desire then to receive training, because they were of the belief that even if they are trained, the white business establishment would still refuse to employ them. Hence the desire to seek out and receive training was nonexistent among the black male.

Again it must be stressed, and I must therefore place great emphasis on the fact that good jobs demand training, skills, and more training. In the past, for example (forty to fifty years ago and beyond), the black man needed a connection in order to get into the business of skilled trades. Today, they need education and training, because there are plenty of skilled jobs for everyone. One of the reasons why the "West Indians," who are the newcomers to America, do so well in their endeavors, as professionals as well as skilled workers, is because they come here (to America) as trained people; either as nurses, doctors, technicians, mechanics, electricians, masons (brick layers) carpenters, commercial drivers, bookkeepers, accountants, beauticians, housekeepers, and many more. In spite of these inherent abilities, these people still find the time to go back to school to learn the American way of doing things in order to advance and improve their skills or professions in the American society. Thus, if one is to achieve the American dream, the emphasis must be placed on getting a good education along with proper training.

(c) PLANNING

Plan your future; formulate a method for achieving your objectives. Make a sketch in your mind of where you went wrong in the past and try to move away from that path. Make an outline of where you are heading and what you want to accomplish. Don't expend your time lamenting on the past "the past is dead and gone."

One writer commented that "man cannot discover new oceans unless he has the courage to lose sight of the shore." But on the other hand, "don't count your chickens before they are hatched...." "The future is not yet born." The time to think of is now, today, but you must plan for tomorrow.

Make the effort, don't just sit there and "wish." Mamie

McCullough said that "success consists of a series of little daily efforts."

Consider all your options, all possibilities, and also the impossibilities. Put your self in the middle of the probabilities. In order to build a house, you need a plan, but the prerequisite to any form of planning is a set of clearly defined goals. Many people never achieve their goals or enjoy success, because they do not have sound planning, nor set goals. Whatever you do, you should have a realistic view of your own ability to do the things which you set out to do.

The 1997 graduate yearbook of Princeton University in New Jersey has the following caption written by one of the graduates:

Togettothenuthousejustcontinueonthedesignatedpath.

(d) FOCUS

To succeed in life, you must imagine in your mind what you want to accomplish. In order to pursue your field of interest, you must concentrate on your goals. Don't flicker or waver in your undertakings. If obstacles develop, adjust your situations and move on. Life's journey is based on adjustment; there is no easy path to success, but you should keep your eyes on what you are aiming for.

Exert yourself, apply some mental and physical energy in whatever you do. High achievements depend on the efforts we made, the drive we have, and the force we apply.

(e) MOTIVATION

There is a close correlation between motivation, education, and success. One of the first principles of high achievement is motivation – the will to get ahead. Hence the propensity to stay in school (and learn), the motivation to graduate, the inclination to find a job (after graduation), to hold on to the job, and to advance yourself in the job.

You must have a vision of what life would be like in the future years if you did not have a high school diploma or a college degree. Discouragement may sometimes dampen your spirit; but don't be discouraged, the road to success is dotted with many tempting parking places.

(f) GOOD WORK ETHIC

One writer remarked, "when excellence becomes tradition, no goal lies out of reach." Always do your best at whatever you do. Be not slothful, avoid tardiness, "he that is faithful in that which is least is also faithful in much." Bible verse.

Work hard at your job; as one Caribbean native (mentioned earlier), remarked, "the American dream is hard work." Don't quit your job before you find another one; leave your options open just in case you have to go back. If you are good at what you do, think about working for yourself. If you need further training, go to a school that specializes in your field of interest. If you need assistance, talk to your teachers, your professors, your classmates, your counselors, and your friends.

The late Vince Lombardi stated that "the price of success is hard work, dedication to the job at hand, and determination that whether we win or lose, we have applied the best of ourselves to the task at hand."

Albert Einstein admonished us on the importance of work as it relates to success in the following algebraic formula: "If 'A' is success in life, then $A = (X+Y+Z)$. Work is X, Y is play, and Z is keeping your mouth shut."

(g) HONESTY

One of the sure way to secure, build, and advance yourself into a career-path is through the medium of honesty and trustworthiness – getting others to believe in you and to trust you can greatly enhance your chance of a successful life.

People can be judged by the things that they say, and by the things that they do. If you say one thing and do another, you could be judged as being dishonest; hence, you must be consistent. I do not know of any big corporation that will promote any employee to a top executive position if they knew that that employee is dishonest and cannot be trusted.

One might ask, what does honesty have to do with success and high achievements? The simple answer is; whether you are an employee or an employer, honesty in all your undertakings is the best policy. Honesty is a manifestation of trustworthiness, truthfulness, integrity, and sincerity.

Deception and prevention are an unpleasant omen in the path of one's goals. Making commitments and fulfilling them, making promises and abiding by them, are fundamental aspects of mutual respects for others.

(h) ATTITUDE

Attitude is a state of mind or feeling with regard to a person or a thing.

Our attitude can be a major stumbling block in our efforts to realize our dreams. Some people have a tendency to react unfavorably towards certain situations, mainly because of their experiences, or out of frustration, caused by the behavior or doings of others towards them. These unfavorable attitudes are especially pronounced among people who have been discriminated against.

Many people lose their privileges in life because of unfavorable attitudes toward other people; for example, their parents, their teachers, their employers, or even their coaches (if they are in sports). Sometimes we are given unpleasant tasks as a testing technique; but the temperamental individual must be careful not to "lose his or her cool."

The most destructive aspect of an individual with bad attitude occurs when unfavorable attitude is demonstrated into words; in many instances the end results are acted out in a physical manner. In any shape or form, bad attitudes are hazardous to our achievements. It appears as if there is a close correlation between the attitudes we manifest (good or bad) and our own emotions, which are also in conflict with our aspirations. Thus unfavorable attitudes, which bring about an emotion of anger and violence, will no doubt prevent and hinder sound reasoning.

(i) BELIEVE IN YOURSELF

Ralph Waldo Emerson penned the following words: "What lies behind us and what lies before us are tiny matters compared to what lies within us." Believe in yourself; think positive; develop self-confidence and self-assurance.

Descartes admonished us; "Conquer yourself rather than the world."

Will Rogers also admonished us, when he stated, "In order to succeed, you must know what you are doing, like what you are doing, and believe in what you are doing."

(j) VISION

Put yourself in the proximity of your dreams; share your views; talk to people who are in the field of your interest. Open up, converse, and seek the advise of people on things that are Germane to your interest and ask how to go about achieving them. Read up on the subject matter. If possible volunteer your service to organizations of that nature.

Think of the short range as well as the long range. Don't be too hasty in your endeavor, take your time. Abraham Lincoln once said, "The best thing about the future is that it comes only one day at a time."

Don't be annoyed if people call you a dreamer; one writer remarked; "It is only with the heart that one can see rightly; what is essential is invisible to the eyes."

Winston Churchill once said, "It is a mistake to look too far ahead," and that "only one link of the chain of destiny can be handled at a time." But oftentimes people lose sight of the future because of the preoccupation of the immediate rewards.

Robert Browning said that "…a man's reach must exceed his grasp, or what is heaven for?"

Finally, basic education and good home training are fundamentally important, and is the foundation of high achievements and a successful career. Many children and young adults who have disobeyed and strayed away from the will and the guidance of their parents (rude, lack discipline, offensive, lewd, loudmouthed, and so on) more than often lack the desire to pursue a successful career. The bible admonishes in Ephesians Chapter 6: Verse 1: "Children obey your parents in the lord: for this is right. Honor thy father and mother that it may be well with thee and thou mayest live long on the earth, Verse 2: The parents are admonished in Proverbs Chapter 22: Verse 6: "Train up a child in the way he should go: and when he is old, he will not depart from it."

* * *